HOW WE
LEARNED TO SKI

William Collins Sons and Co Ltd
London · Glasgow · Sydney · Auckland
Toronto · Johannesburg

© Ali Ross and Harold Evans 1983
First published 1983

Designed by Graham Davis
Set in Egyptian Light
Made and Printed in Great Britain
by W. S. Cowell Ltd,
Ipswich, Suffolk

Ross, Ali
How we learned to ski.
1. Skis and skiing
I. Title   II. Evans, Harold, 1928
796.93   GV854

ISBN 0 00 217164 3

HOW WE LEARNED TO SKI

ALI ROSS AND HAROLD EVANS

COLLINS
8 Grafton Street, London W1
in association with Peter Stuyvesant Travel
1983
in association with Channel Four Television Company Ltd

CONTENTS

ALI ROSS GURU OF THE TELEVISION SERIES

It's inhuman not to feel envious when you see Ali Ross swoop down a glacier in Switzerland, or snake through the larch trees in the Rockie mountains of Colorado in a plume of light powder snow. Try another image. A young boy in Strathpeffer in the Highlands of Scotland rips a couple of planks from his father's shed, nails his father's wellington boots to the planks, climbs through the snow to the top of a large hill, puts feet in wellies – and catapults forward in a tremendous fall as the fronts of the home-made skis dig into the slope.

Everybody has to begin somewhere, everybody learns that falling need not be very frightening. And everybody beginning to ski today has a better start than young Ross on his wellie-planks. The skis, the boots and the bindings which hold boot to ski are all on our side, and so, mostly, is the teaching.

We were 25 years too late to film that bold beginning to the career of Ali Ross, ski teacher, when we made a series of six documentaries for Channel 4 Television in 1983 entitled *How We Learned to Ski.* But we followed every minute of his teaching over six weeks and this book is the story of how all his pupils learned – and how almost anyone can learn – to ski well enough to enjoy a little speed, a little solitude and a great sense of adventure. If you missed the TV series, this book can be read on its own (though a teaching cassette is also available from Peter Stuyvesant Travel*). It is the essence of the Ali Ross teaching method. Where 'I' occurs in the text it is Ali speaking. Elsewhere, the words should be read as our joint work.

It is possible to pick up ski-ing quite quickly. I offer myself as some kind of example. I was 42 before I tried on a pair of skis on a dry slope. I went to Austria and was bewildered by the amount of balletically precise things I had to do simultaneously with thighs, elbows, arms, shoulders, hips, knees and nostrils; and by skis which rose 18″ over my head. Out of frustration I started to write a book with my

*35 Alfred Place, London WC1E 7DY. £16.95 (inc. packaging and postage)

colleagues Brian Jackman and Mark Ottaway of *The Sunday Times*. It took two years to produce *We Learned to Ski* in 1974 but when we had finished it we really had learned to ski any mountain, and powder, and at reasonable speed.

Evans, Jackman and Ottaway owe a lot of their progress to Ali Ross. Aged 40 now, he has taught thousands to ski in 21 years. For the last 11 years he has been based at the Ski School at Wengen in Switzerland, and the Downhill Only Club send him their young racers to train. He holds a Grade I certification from the British Association of Ski Instructors and was our natural choice for instructor when Channel 4 agreed to a proposition, from Goldcrest Films and Television, that our original book should become a documentary series.

The idea was that we would take groups of beginners, intermediates, and advanced skiers, turn them over to Ali Ross and film what happened. We were four weeks at Wengen in Switzerland and two at Vail in Colorado with a brilliant director, Marek Kanievska, and two prodigious cameramen, Jon Lane from Britain and Roger Brown from Colorado, and a skiing crew. We had Stefan Zurcher and Rene Seiler to

ski special sequences — Zurcher was the Russian baddie in the Bond film who zoomed over a cowshed.

This book, complementary to the big original *We Learned to Ski*, can be squashed in somewhere with your sandwiches and piste map, and looked at again when you take a breather in a sunny mountain restaurant on one of the many magic journeys you will make as a skier.

Harold Evans

(Executive Producer, *How We Learned to Ski*)
Director, Goldcrest

9

FIVE PEOPLE AT THE BOTTOM OF A MOUNTAIN

Three of our beginners had never been on skis before. They all had the same difficulties on the first day coping with the paraphernalia you need to travel about a ski resort.

At first there seems too much to remember and you are bound to leave something behind. So have a mental checklist and count things off one by one: skis, yes; poles, yes; gloves, yes; sunglasses, yes; lift-pass, yes; suncream, yes. And what else? Well, what about money? And a hat for bad weather? And goggles in case it snows? And a piste map? That's a list of 10 items. Take your time, count everything in place before moving downhill.

Good resorts have marker poles at frequent intervals, coloured to the grade of the run and numbered so that you can see where you are. Normally numbers run down from the top to No. 1 at the bottom, and the easiest runs are usually marked green. After green, the next easiest is blue, and then difficult runs: red for advanced intermed - iates and above, black for experts only.

Watch the colours. Sometimes runs cross and if you're not careful you find you have moved from blue to black. A red run might look easy but round the corner there will be a steep gully or a mogul field .

'I'm Jeremy. I've never been on skis before. I'm 27 years of age, 5' 9", and reckon I have a chance at this sport against the bigger guys.'

'I'm Junri. I'm 24, I left Japan when I was four years old and I'm studying law. I had a bad experience trying to learn some years ago; now I'm ready to try again.'

'I'm Melanie, 23, and 5' 5". This is my first time ski-ing, though I can water-ski. I soon learned not to worry about taking a tumble.'

'I'm Keith, aged 32 and 6' 4". I'd been warned by other skiers that my size would be a problem but I didn't really appreciate how unnerving it would be in the first few days, trying to coordinate a long-limbed, heavy body and feel in control on a sliding base.'

'I'm Virginia, a writer from Sydney. I'm 38 and determined that's not too old to learn. All I've done before, 20 years ago, is have a four-day session in Austria, but I play tennis, swim, climb trees — and run up escalators.'

COPING WITH YOUR FEELINGS

Let's face the biggest problem of learning to ski at once. Keith put it candidly: 'It really does strike fear into your heart to stand at the top of what seems, early on, to be a steep, bumpy slope when you haven't done it before.'

It's only by recognizing the nature of your fears that you can hope to progress. First, it is very natural that the urban dweller, used to flat, concrete areas, should be disturbed by the space and drama of the mountains: it's easy to have images of hurtling off a rocky cliff in a blizzard. In fact, skis areas, and certainly beginners' areas, are very carefully selected so that precipices are not readily to hand when you slide away. If Keith fell at the top of that slope he would soon come to a stop.

The second fear is injury. The risks have dropped sharply because modern bindings release the foot before any leverage of the ski can break a bone or tear a ligament; of course, it is vital that the bindings are adjusted properly. A commoner risk today is of collision. Ski considerately, never out of control, never stand in the middle of the traffic. Even so injury must be kept in perspective. The worldwide average is that we risk injury once in 400 days of ski-ing. Insurers reckon that two weeks at the seaside are about as risky as one week's ski-ing.

A third fear is of not doing well, of looking silly. Forget it! You are there to enjoy yourself — and ultimately to teach yourself. Too many become over-dependent on their teachers, vulnerable to chance remarks. You learn best when you take the information and advice, understand it and translate it to your own use.

I feel strongly that I don't teach people: people learn. Part of this learning process is awareness of what is happening to you. Think about that and don't just do movements in a robot-like daze. Don't expect to get anything right first or fifth time. Be patient.

The first few days are vital in building skills for the future. Spend time at this; don't expect to go rushing about the mountain at once. When you find yourself getting tense and disappointed, stop and have a look around the mountains and remember why you are there. That usually puts everything right.

ENVIRONMENT

The ultimate in ski-ing is to be able to travel everywhere on the mountain, from the gentle nursery slope to something like this, reached only by helicopter. Here is Ali Ross, at 3,058m (10,000ft) on the glacier, the Eigergletscher, which runs east from the Eiger above Wengen, in Switzerland. It is hazardous ski-ing between the seracs with uncertain snow and dangerous crevasses. Ali always goes with companions, often the Wengen experts Stefan Zurcher and Rene Seiler.

ENVIRONMENT: IT DOES SNOW SOMETIMES

Windchill is something to which beginners never really pay enough attention. Look at this example. A normal temperature in still air conditions at the top of an alpine mountain is 20°F — that's 12° of frost. If you are moving at 15 mph that reduces the temperature to −6°F or 38° of frost. When you add the chill from even a 15 mph headwind, the temperature will be down to −18°F. That's 50° of frost.

This is Marek Kanievska, the director of *How We Learned to Ski*, on a March day in Wengen. People were bowled over by the force of the blizzards. Never, never underestimate the mountains and their capacity for surprise.

On the second day of our filming we started off under hot blue skies. In ten minutes, around noon, it changed to heavy snow and it was cold. Filming the intermediates one day we left the village with people in shirtsleeves, and up the mountain found ourselves in a 35-40 mph wind and sub-zero temperatures; and one of the men had left his hat behind. I try to keep my group ski-ing in this weather, if only to keep warm, but if people are doing badly, I go inside for a coffee. There's no point in making everyone miserable.

There are three conditions that the skier has to cope with — temperature, snow and visibility. Proper clothing is the answer on temperature, and we deal with it shortly.

Snow varies according to the time of day, season, the angle of the mountain, and the way it accumulated in the first place. What every skier soon learns is that on cold mornings and north-facing slopes, especially when there has been wind, you will get icy routes or sheets of ice. Your skis must have sharp edges. Check them regularly.

The opposite condition is porridge, slush, or mashed potato, which beginners find hard to turn in and which you look out for on the lower slopes and especially when the sun has been out in spring. When facing slush I took the TV beginners along shadier edges where there was still good snow. In between these two conditions is crust, a layer of ice on top of spring or powder snow. If it breaks easily it is similar to ski-ing in spring snow; when it is thicker and erratic in breaking it tests the best skiers.

Sometimes in a white-out, visibility is so bad you can see nothing. A more general condition is an overcast day with low cloud and no sun coming through to cast shadows. This diffused light means you cannot see bumps and dips. I go slower then. As I told the TV group, I aim to take advantage of this by trying to *feel* more. That idea seemed to help.

Windchill Equivalent Temperatures (degrees F)

Calm	35°	30°	25°	20°	15°	10°	5°	0°	−5°	−10°	−15°	−20°
5	33°	27°	21°	16°	12°	7°	1°	−6°	−11°	−15°	−20°	−26°
10	21°	16°	9°	2°	−2°	−9°	−15°	−22°	−27°	−31°	−38°	−45°
15	16°	11°	1°	−6°	−11°	−18°	−25°	−33°	−40°	−45°	−51°	−60°
20	12°	3°	−4°	−9°	−17°	−24°	−32°	−40°	−46°	−52°	−60°	−68°
25	7°	0°	−7°	−15°	−22°	−29°	−37°	−45°	−52°	−58°	−67°	−75°
30	5°	−2°	−11°	−18°	−26°	−33°	−41°	−49°	−56°	−63°	−70°	−78°
35	3°	−4°	−13°	−20°	−27°	−35°	−43°	−52°	−60°	−67°	−72°	−83°
	Little Danger		Increasing Danger									
			Flesh may freeze within 1 minute									

WHAT THE WELL-DRESSED SKIER WEARS

I liked the way most of my TV groups dressed. They were dressed for the mountains — and they looked attractive. There is no reason why sense and style should not go together. Anyone who skis in snow wearing jeans, of course, is a conceited fool. It means 'I don't fall', but who can be so sure? And nobody can tell what weather the mountains will produce to make the show-off a hospital case of exposure.

Even experienced skiers make blunders here. When I met the advanced group in Vail one morning they were all cold — they'd looked out of the hotel window and seen sunshine, and thought that meant warmth. But whereas the temperature may have been about 25°F at the bottom, at the mountaintop, allowing for height, movement and wind, the temperature was about −18°F (see windchill chart on p.16). I really recommend taking a rucksack for spare clothing and equipment.

My main complaint is against the sale of ski clothes with material that slips on the snow. It's crazy. Ski-ing is a falling down sport. Everyone falls. I do. You will. Normally you will not slide far, certainly not at beginner speeds, but as you go faster you need clothing to slow you down, not make you a projectile. Check the labels. Non-slip material is usually identified. Beware the shiny nylons.

But let's start from the skin. Longjohns made of silk keep you warm in the cold and cool in the sun. Next a T-shirt and possibly a sweater: several layers of light clothing keep in warmth. My own preference is for a suit lined with Thinsulate thermal insulation. It's a new material made by 3M and for the same thickness provides nearly twice the thermal resistance of materials such as down, fibrefill, pile or wool. Thinsulate fibres absorb less than 1% of their weight in water so you can stay warm even after falls in wet slush.

So much for the lining. The outer material is no more than showerproof in most ski gear. If you are in the rain for an hour you get wet. The suit I wear is made of a new, completely waterproof fabric called Goretex. The remarkable thing is that I get no condensation inside. These materials have made my life easier.

I prefer a single-piece suit or salopette overalls: it means I don't get snow down my front or back when I fall in the deeper stuff. Look for a tight cuff round the wrist so that when the glove is on there is nowhere for snow to penetrate. The collar should come up around the ears and stay there, by zip or press-stud, when you are moving fast in a high wind.

Top it all off with a good hat which has earpieces or will pull down over your ears: they're very sensitive to cold and altitude. A bare head allows a large amount of body heat to dissipate: when you're hot, take off your hat.

You cannot go up the mountain even briefly without protection for *eyes* and *skin*: the ultra-violet radiation is stronger than at the seaside. Even when you cannot see the sun, the light in the mountains is powerful and the snow reflects it.

It's not vital to get the very best sunglasses, though good quality, shatterproof lenses are obviously sensible; but it is vital that you keep glasses on. I never cease to wonder at people who worry about going home with 'panda eyes' than they do about their eyesight.

Goggles are needed in bad light and snowfalls. I have come across a lot of people in misery without them. Get double lens goggles, which mist up less easily. Keep a pocket full of dry tissues or a piece of chamois leather to keep them dry.

Finally, skin. Yes, I know you want a suntan, but for the first few days, at least, cover exposed skin with a suncream having a protection factor of at least 6 (they run from around 2 to about 15/18). Put cream on parts of your face that normally miss the sun, like under the chin, under the nose, under the eyebrows, the eyelids and the bottoms of the ears and the neck. Don't be misled because you don't feel the sun burning you. The amount of burn is concealed by the coolness of the air and the fact that some of the sun's rays are reflected from cold snow.

Nothing less than a total blocking cream (like Lavia Sun) or a lipstick (Lipsalve) will do for the lips — and use them from Day One. It's sad to see people applying cream to swollen lip blisters when it's too late.

That is the story of surviving happily as a skier — a stitch in time.

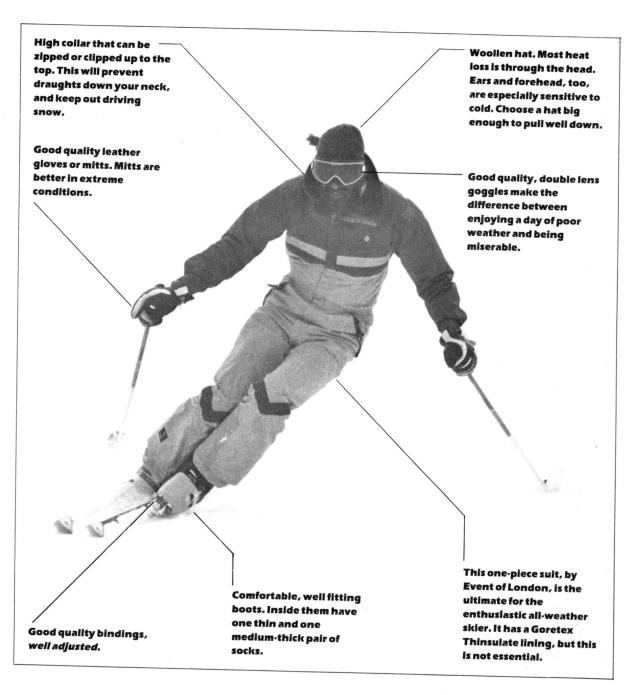

High collar that can be zipped or clipped up to the top. This will prevent draughts down your neck, and keep out driving snow.

Good quality leather gloves or mitts. Mitts are better in extreme conditions.

Woollen hat. Most heat loss is through the head. Ears and forehead, too, are especially sensitive to cold. Choose a hat big enough to pull well down.

Good quality, double lens goggles make the difference between enjoying a day of poor weather and being miserable.

Good quality bindings, well adjusted.

Comfortable, well fitting boots. Inside them have one thin and one medium-thick pair of socks.

This one-piece suit, by Event of London, is the ultimate for the enthusiastic all-weather skier. It has a Goretex Thinsulate lining, but this is not essential.

19

ENVIRONMENT: SOMETHING FOR EVERYONE

There is a marvellous range of resorts to choose from in Europe and in the United States; they are analyzed in *We Learned to Ski*.

Put very simply there are three kinds in Europe. There are pre-Alpine resorts which are low, usually below 1,400m (4,600ft) but with lifts to higher slopes. Many Austrian resorts are in this category. You'll see two figures in the brochure and in the list at the back of this book: one is the height of the town and the other of the highest lift.

The traditional Alpine resorts are higher (up to 1,834m or 6,000ft, say), again with access to higher mountains. Many of the Swiss and Italian resorts are like this.

Finally, there are the new purpose-built resorts, chiefly in France and the United States, but also in Spain, where you ski and sleep nearer the top of the mountain.

Wengen, where we made four of our films, is a Swiss village in the Bernese Oberland at 1,276m (4,187ft) with the top lift at 2,320m (7,000ft). You ski under the Eiger and the Jungfrau. The modern sport began in Wengen and in Murren, across the valley, developed by the mad British who carried their skis up the mountain. It took a little persuasion to convince the Swiss that the summer railway should be opened when there was snow on the ground...Today Wengen thrives but retains a secluded charm. Care and conservation have preserved the natural beauty; there are no cars in the village.

Vail in Colorado, where we shot the advanced skiing, was a sheep meadow in 1962. In 1963, when no snow was in sight, Minnie Cloud and Southern Ute Indian dancers performed a snow dance. The resort opened with one and a half feet...Now it is a major resort with chair-lifts starting from your hotel door. We stayed at The Lodge and when we swam in the pool at the end of the day we could watch the last of the skiers descend into the sunset. Superb broad trails have been cut in the White River National Forest starting at 2,446m (8,000ft) with a summit of 3,440m (11,250ft) and there are huge 'back bowls' for powder ski-ing. The Rockies are rightly famous for their powder snow; Vail now has 16 miles of pipes to carry artificial snow if there is a bad season.

ENVIRONMENT: SOMETHING FOR EVERYONE

You can ski through rolling, wooded hills, or broad, gentle meadows, or way above the tree line on wide bare slopes with jagged peaks all around. The Alpine tree line ranges from 1,800m (5,900ft) to 2,000m (6,500ft); in the Rockies we skied through pine and larch woods at 3,058m (10,000ft).

The drama of the terrain is not necessarily a reliable guide to the difficulty of the ski-ing: one of the pleasantest and easiest runs in Wengen is below the face of the Eiger to Brandegg.

The big open slopes above the tree line offer fewer obstacles, but trees help skiers: the visibility is better and the snow is retained longer. This may be important when high winds have removed much of the cover on higher open ground.

Some of the more difficult patches in any resort may be near home, where skiers making turns in the same spot have produced a concentration of the bumps known as moguls, with maybe rocks and bare roots exposed in awkward spots.

Many runs towards the resort follow narrow mountain tracks winding through woods, with an ice wall on one side and a sharp incline on the other. But generally these mountain tracks have little gradient and can be skied with ease (the biggest hazard tends to be other skiers going a shade too fast).

Ski-ing should begin on nursery slopes with little gradient and a flat area for you to run out safely, without having to worry about gathering speed. It's crazy to start anywhere else. When we were making our film we saw a party of Japanese beginners falling all over the place as they attempted to start on a fairly steep slope near the top. You can be sure few will return to ski-ing.

At Wengen we took the train to our play area. It may seem tame at first.

'It's very annoying just to be walking around and doing nothing,' said Melanie. But she was doing something. She was getting the feel of her skis.

I cannot stress too much how valuable this is. You can play around on the nursery slopes without needing anyone to tell you what to do — we'll come to some of the exercises later.

Build your confidence.

Keith and Melanie on an easy homeward path through the woods. The main hazard is other skiers coming round the corner. 'I'd make them wear flashing lights and sirens,' said Melanie.

All (top right) in a mogul field — fun later on in your ski career but not for beginners.

Keith (bottom right) on a green run (and hanging back too much).

ENVIRONMENT: THE LIFTS

We got to the top in Wengen by railway and cable-car. But ski-ing around Wengen, or Zermatt, say, which is also served by a railway, you use other systems as well.

There are the Pomma lift for one skier; the T-bar for two skiers; single, double and sometimes triple chair-lifts; the gondola or bubble-car holding four people; and the cable-car taking 40 or 50.

You take your skis off to travel by rail, cable-car or gondola, but keep them on for the chair-lift and the other drag-lifts.

In choosing a resort, always ask for a transport map, both for mountain service and proximity to where you are staying.

Half a mile from a lift is half a mile carrying skis at the end of the day. If the only way to the top is by drag-lift, it means tiring journeys and probably queues, depending on the number of lifts and bottleneck points.

Maps give the lift length and vertical rise so you can judge how steep or long they are: a tow longer than a kilometre (3,280ft) is worth missing. But note that purpose-built French resorts are high up the mountain to start with, unlike older resorts in valley villages and towns.

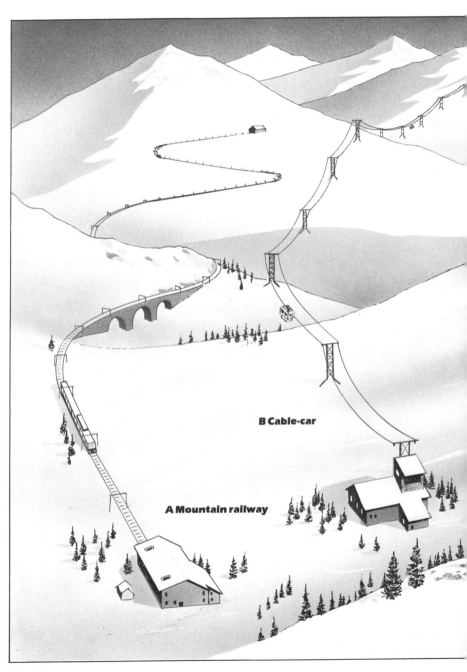

B Cable-car

A Mountain railway

C T-bar

D Telecabine

E Chair-lift

ON THE MOVE: RIDING THE LIFTS

A run on the mountain will normally take you to the bottom of a lift where you can expect to join a queue. It is not like being in a normal queue because the skis protrude forwards, and you will get black looks if you let your tips slip on to the tails of the skier in front.

Everyone finds the T-bar for two the trickiest lift to ride. This is what you do . . .

Getting on: Agree with your partner who goes to the far side. Move as soon as the previous pair depart. Assume the right waiting position, facing uphill with skis apart, poles in the outside hand. There should be a low checkboard behind, against which you can push the tails of your skis: then you know you are in a good position. Turn your head and grab the T-bar as it comes at you . . . but don't sit down on it. The bar is not a chair, it is only a means of having you dragged uphill. As the T-bar takes up your pressure, simply stand up and let it pull.

Going up: It's like ski-ing uphill with the power of the lift replacing gravity. So assume your normal position for straight running, knees slightly bent. We have a scene in one of our television programmes of two of the big intermediate skiers, Jim and Corey, fighting hard all the way up the mountain to stay with the T-bar. The mistake they had made was to allow their boots to push against each other, taking them off-centre and calling for great muscular strength to stay on-track. The trick is to push shoulder to shoulder while keeping the weight on both feet. No leaning. Weight on both skis.

It can be tricky following the tracks up the slope, especially in the mornings when the sun has not had time to melt overnight ice. Keep your knees flexed. Bend to absorb the bumps, stretch in the hollows. Drag lifts often have short patches where they go downhill, which can be alarming at first as you gather speed. Edge the skis in a small plough to slow down.

After a few successful rides it is easy to daydream. That is the moment there is a nasty rut in the track or your partner changes weight on a ski or your ski runs across his, and you're off. Move quickly out of the way of the following skiers.

Getting off: As you arrive at the top, there's a small acceleration and you pull yourself forward slightly to get off the hook of the T-bar. Take care not to do that too soon before your skis are over the incline. Skiers often linger at the exit of the T-bar, which is hazardous: the T-bar, once released, swings around a lot. Move to a safer place.

The pomma or button-lift: This works on the same principle as the T-bar, but it is for a single skier. A metal pole is attached to the cable going up the mountain. There is a button the size of a teaplate at the end of the pole and you place this between your legs. Some pomma -lifts have quite a violent tug at the beginning, so take care. At the end of the ride, pull down on the pole to release the button.

The chair-lift: This gave our group one or two heartskips, mainly because of awkwardness with the poles. Take your hands out of your ski straps and hold both poles in one hand – the one to the outside of the chair-lift.

You and your partner must decide before the chair arrives who will go to the far side. As soon as the previous chair has gone, move into position. Look over your shoulder as the chair comes at you and sit down in the chair as the edge of it just about strikes the rear of your knees. Your free hand holds on to the bar supporting the chair.

This is the point at which someone drops sticks, gloves, glasses, lift-pass. Forget them. Lift crews are used to that and will send the article up with the next passengers. If you are ski-ing with a child they will slow the lift for you.

Once in the moving chair, and when you are both ready for it, pulled down a metal 'gate' over your head; this holds you in the chair and usually offers a footrest for the skis. Raise your ski tips as you move off because often there is an awkward pile of snow at the take-off point. Do the same again as you approach the snow ramp at the end of the ride.

You leave the chair – having raised the 'gate' – by sliding the skis on the ramp, standing up and letting yourself go down the slight incline. Then get out of the way of the next pair.

Only the older European resorts have mountain railways. Most big jumps up the mountain are by **cable - car** where you stand up, jammed in with others carrying skis as you sway up the mountain. Cable - cars are not as comfortable as the bubble, gondola or **telecabine** where two or four sit down.

These major lifts are all simple to use, though the clatter and the crush remind you of rush hour.

A Mountain railway

B Cable-car

C T-bar

D Telecabine

E Chair-lift

ARE YOU REALLY ALL SET TO GO?

Melanie was honest about it on the second day of our film: 'I've been annoyed with my goggles, angry with my hat, tetchy with the film crew, and what's really wrong is that I didn't realize that it's hard work in a strange environment.' Melanie is a water-skier and windsurfer, fitter than most beginners.

Ski writers tend to say it's the fault of the teaching that 20% who start to ski never continue. I would like to try to spread a little of the blame for this drop-out rate. Travel firms paint a picture of sunny skies and effortless fun. And I'd put some blame on people who arrive mentally and physically unprepared for mountains.

Ski fitness needs special preparation. I do have sympathy with beginners here. A few years ago I spent the whole summer sailing, using my arms and upper body a lot. I thought I was fit. But when I got back on the slopes I couldn't complete some of my favourite runs; my legs were not up to it. So I give some special exercises on these pages for muscles and general suppleness.

Anything to improve cardio-vascular condition is good. The muscles we use ski-ing are different but slow, gentle downhill jogging is a good start — gentle because unexercised muscles and knee joints need care.

We have to remember the arm muscles, too. As Keith said, the mad skier syndrome is a man running up and down stairs to get his legs in trim, but it was Keith's arms that ached at first.

My own fitness training includes hill walking in Scotland, and in London cycling in Richmond Park. That gets the legs in shape. (I fly a hang glider and so carry 90lbs of equipment up the mountain, but I'm not suggesting everyone does that!)

In all our exercises, we should train for awareness of what our bodies are doing at any specific moment. I give myself ten-minute awareness exercises. When I run I imagine ski positions and assume them as I go down a slope, doing slaloms between trees.

A great proportion of ski-ing injuries are fatigue-related; these exercises will increase your stamina and if you follow the sequence say three times a week for about eight weeks before ski-ing you'll arrive fit — and stay that way.

Side stretch
Hands over your head, gently but firmly move out to the side, down towards the floor. Hold for a few seconds then do the same on the other side. Repeat.

Thigh stretch
Do this one only when your body has warmed up. Lean against something stable for balance. Hold one ankle and pull its leg up behind you. Hold for 20 seconds then do the same with the other leg. Repeat.

Leg stretch
Clasp your hands round one shin, stretch the other leg out as straight behind you as you can, pushing against the resistance of your arms and other leg. Feel the stretch and hold for a few seconds.

Crouch walking
Keep as low as possible and keep in balance. Now walk around till your legs burn. Rest a bit and do it again. Build up slowly to 5 walkabouts.

Sit-ups
These can be modified by kicking your legs or twisting your body as you sit up.

Rotation
Feet apart for balance, slowly move your shoulders, circling out from your hips.

More rotation
Hands behind the head, move your shoulders and head in a circle, first one way, then the other. Repeat several times.

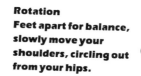

Springer
Feet apart for balance, crouch fairly low with arms set for diving. Then spring to your full height. Repeat several times.

Rest and relax
Stretch down gently to your feet – don't jerk. Straighten up and repeat. To finish off, with head down shake your arms and shoulders like a dog coming out of water.

SKIS AND BOOTS

**Beginners should never accept a pair of skis taller than themselves: they usually need a wider compact ski.
Intermediates or anyone of tall, heavy build would do best with a mid-ski. Experts use the narrower regular ski.**

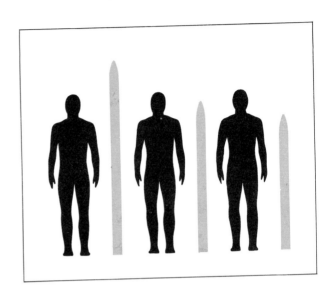

I put four of the beginners in the TV series on compact skis, and one of them, Keith, on a mid-ski. I will explain these terms shortly. Ski manufacturers these days are always experimenting, so I won't go into details of trade names and brand models. *We Learned to Ski* is updated to deal with changes in ski technology, and magazines report as well.

Let us, therefore, keep things simple and say that for the recreational skier, who has different requirements from the downhill racers of *Ski Sunday*, there are three types of ski: the conventional, the mid-ski and the compact.

Everyone used to ski on the conventional ski, anything in length from 170cm to 210cm. It supports weight, it travels fast and it has other qualities which make it suitable for quick turns in which the skier rides on the edge of the ski. However, beginners find it hard to make the long conventional ski turn, are insecure on its narrow base and disenchanted with its quality of speed.

The revolution has been the introduction of the compact ski. This is not only short (150cm to 190cm) but it has a different design: it may be 5mm or more broader at the waist.

I always put beginners and slower or older intermediates on a compact ski. They find it easier to turn and generally easier to manage. It should not be more than head height.

A very heavy person needs a longer ski to support his weight. Keith weighs about 12½ stone (175lbs) and is well over 6ft, so I put him on a longer ski — a mid-ski, a compromise in design between the compact and the conventional ski.

Almost as important as the style of ski is its condition. The steel edges should be kept sharp. That helps them to grip into hard snow and hold you in climbing movements on the hill.

Secondly, the running surface of the ski should be kept flat. Skis become concave or convex with use and even for beginners it is worth having them

Most modern bindings have an upwards release at the heel and a sideways release at the toe. 'Elastic' bindings allow some movement at toe and heel before releasing entirely. A correctly adjusted toe-piece should not press down on the lip of the boot — if it does friction delays release. The most convenient bindings are those which can be removed by pressing down on the heel-piece with a ski pole.

flat-filed in the ski shop. In spring ski-ing, too, the running surface is easily marked by striking a rock or exposed root: never walk along a gravelly road in skis, as some do.

Boots

Comfort counts. All modern boots provide good support. Beginners should hire boots at home and walk around in them over a couple of weeks. There is nothing worse than ill-fitting boots, so take your time getting a good fit, however many people may be waiting in the shop. There should be no pressure anywhere: even a wrinkle in a sock can provide that.

When you are in the boot flex forward from the knee and check that there is no heel lift. You should, however, be able to wriggle your toes. We used Salomon rear-entry boots for our beginners in the film; they were found to be excellent. They hold the foot in the forward position for ski-ing but have a clip that can be loosened so that you can walk in them.

Melanie and Jeremy still got sore shins from their boots, cured with shin pads.

Bindings

These hold boots to skis. Most safety bindings are designed to release the foot on a sideways twist and for the heel to lift out of the binding under pressure. Nothing is more vital in ski-ing than understanding your bindings. Get them set in the shop so that they release under the proper pressure. I see too many accidents because people have screwed their own bindings too tight.

Poles

What matters is the right length. In the shop turn it upside down and hold it immediately below the basket. With elbows tucked into your side, your arm should be parallel to the ground. Choose poles with loop straps at the top of the handle; these allow you to vary your grip without losing the pole.

ARTIFICIAL SKI SLOPES

Yes to plastic for all classes of skier. A list of dry slopes is at the back of this book. They are, of course, almost everything that ski-ing is not. They are restricted, the surface may be muddy, they don't give the same sensation as snow, and they are unpleasant in a fall. But all the negative points end abruptly there.

Beginners
People who arrive in the ski resort without benefit of any practice on a dry slope waste four to five days of an expensive holiday.

I recommend an average of four one-hour dry training sessions – there's no point in more than an hour at a time – and I find that beginners who have had dry practice are mentally and physically better prepared, and can exploit their enthusiasm. Others keenly get into boots for about 8 hours a day and often find skin around the ankles or on the shins will not take the strain; they may lose at least three days off the skis. Dry slope practice is worth it for that acclimatization alone.

But one word to dry-slopers. Even though you may have managed quite well on the plastic, treat yourself as a total beginner when you arrive in the resort. Snow is different. It is quicker. That makes it easier for turning, but get used to it. Consolidate your skill. You will advance all the quicker if you begin with humility.

Intermediates
Most ski schools want people to move round the mountain fairly soon, and that is popular. But it means that basic techniques can be skimped. Go 'dry' to polish them.

Advanced
On a two-week holiday, when the sun shines and the snow is beautiful, you don't feel like half a day in ski school improving basic skills. You want to move, and don't want to be told you are doing something not quite right. Understandable. Improve back home on the dry slope. I have run successful clinics for advanced skiers, working on skills that can be adapted from plastic to deep snow. Every advanced skill, including bump ski-ing, can be improved on the plastic.

Sarah Lewis, one of our best young racers in the British national team, learned most of her basic techniques on plastic.

HAVE SKIS, WILL TRAVEL

Jon Lane, the first unit cameraman, caught a perfect moment in the opening stages of the first TV programme. Virginia (*below*) has her skis on her shoulder at the railway station in Wengen and she wings round to put them into the special trunk. Klonk! The tails of her skis catch another skier in the back. He is not amused. It is a perfect moment, of course, only in the sense that it is a spontaneous demonstration of a common error and one not confined to beginners.

This is how you carry your skis easily and safely.

Stand the skis upright with the flat running surfaces face to face. Clip on a couple of cheap ski straps. (Many skiers find a way of making the skis adhere without these, by sliding one ski against another so that the safety catch holds them together.)

Raise the skis to left or right shoulder with the tips to your front. There's a point where they balance naturally on your shoulder, normally just in front of the toe of the bindings, so that the whole bindings plate is at your back. Don't attempt to carry skis with the bindings sticking in your shoulder: it's excruciating. Yet I've seen scores of beginners gritting teeth and doing just that.

When the skis are balanced on your shoulder, hold the tips down towards the chest as I'm doing on top of the mountain. I haven't bothered to carry the skis

I carry the skis with tips forward, tails raised, both poles in one hand usefully poised to help me up a hill or to stay steady on an icy street.

Stepping in: toe first, heel raised. But the boot must have no snow on its base.

scraping boot sole on binding. A more certain method is to balance on one leg with one pole, and prise the snow off with the spike of the other.

Never neglect this. The foot must be flat in the binding. Snow under the sole affects the release mechanism and could keep your leg in the binding under too much pressure for muscle and bone.

You step into most modern bindings and they close under heel pressure. Make sure the heelpiece is raised, then step in, toe first, heel slightly raised. The heel snaps down to close the heelpiece on the rear rim of the boot.

Straps and Stoppers

What happens when you are ski-ing and the boot comes out of the binding? The ski could run away from you – disaster for you, danger for others. That should not happen because most skis nowadays are fitted with a ski-stopper, a strip of metal which is released on a spring and digs into the snow the moment your foot comes out. Some rental skis may not be fitted with a ski-stopper, however. Then you should make sure that there is a retaining strap to hold ski and boot together.

Classes

Take lessons. There are some very good ski teachers who have benefited, as we all have, from attempts to analyze what we do, and even the average teacher will help you to find your way around.

The first time you go to an area, even as an advanced skier, go out with a class or a guide: you can learn so much in one day with a good guide to make the rest of the holiday a lot more fun. On the first day or two, anyway, assign yourself modestly.

Avoid large groups. You get very little ski-ing, let alone teaching, in a group as large as 15. It's better to experiment on the nursery slopes or to ski in a class you think below your standard.

Beginners who start to do well should beware friends, husbands and wives encouraging to join them on the 'easy' red run. I've known scores of cases where people progressing well have been set back by other skiers failing to realize just how much they themselves have learned.

In a class, don't do anything you cannot understand. Ask. There's no shame in it.

flat, though most people find it more comfortable. You can walk for miles with skis in this position. And when you put the skis down, look around.

In some crowded areas you cannot carry skis this way. Over a very short distance you can carry them vertically by gripping them just above the toe bindings, with the tips uppermost.

The Big Moment

Check that the running surfaces of the skis are free of grit or ice. Stand the ski poles in the snow within reach. Place the skis on the flat, side by side. An amazing number of beginners try to get into skis when they are on a surface that is not quite flat. Charlie Chaplin comedies result.

Wait for it ... Always make sure that there is no snow on the sole of the boot. In certain snow conditions it can take several minutes to knock off the snow. You can do it by banging boot on boot or by

BASIC SKILLS: WALKING AND CLIMBING

At last you are moving on snow. Always begin on friendly ground. Our TV five were full of enthusiasm – and full of aches and pains the next day after about four hours on snow. Shins, feet, shoulders, knees, all felt the strain.

So take it easy. I'd advise beginners to take their first three or four days as a half day at a time – no more than two hours on snow unless you have had a lot of dry slope practice. You can do a lot in two hours. In our four hours we learned to walk around, climb a small hill, and slide down it. Here are the very basic moves.

Walking
The only thing in common with ordinary walking is that you push one foot forward after another. But on skis you do not lift the foot. Slide, slide, slide . . .

Try to get a sort of glide going along the length of the ski. Don't worry about pole and arm coordination at this stage. Just keep sliding forward with a natural push on the poles.

Most of us, when we stand still, have our feet splayed at about five to one, ten to two. Translated to skis this gives us a position where the tips of the skis are about two feet apart and the tails close together. Wrong! Try to slide the skis forward in parallel. The adjustment is

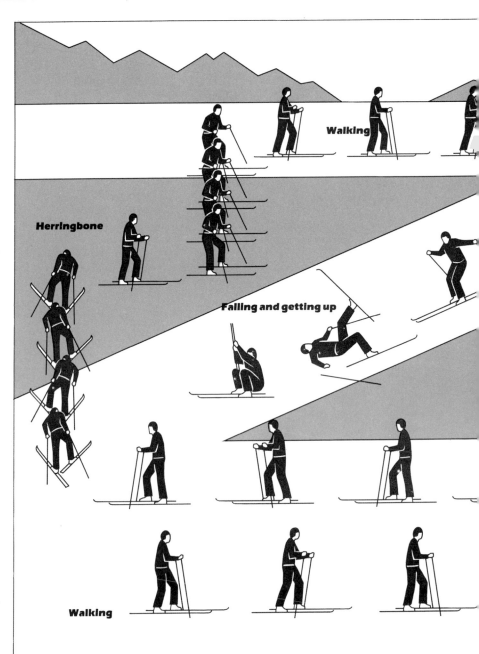

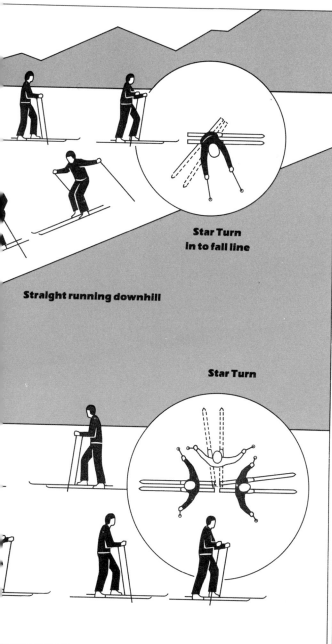

Straight running downhill

**Star Turn
in to fall line**

Star Turn

soon made.

Star turn: Imagine the skis are the hands of a clock and step round without crossing one ski on another.

Climbing

Try the sidestep first. This is the first time you use the edges of the skis. Stand sideways to the slope, with knees pressed forward and sideways into the hill so that the skis are on the uphill edges. This stops them sliding.

Lift a ski and place it half a yard or less up the slope, still with knees pressed into the hill. Next, plant one pole downhill, push off from it, and step up with the second ski (keep it a few inches away from the uphill ski). Repeat.

Next, the herringbone — more effort and only possible on a modest slope. Place the poles behind you for a good push off. Form a wide V with ski-tips apart. Bend the knees and turn them inwards so that you are resting on the inside edges of the ski. Push off from the poles, one ski at a time, setting it down once again on its inside edge. This stops you sliding back.

**Top: Although one feels clumsy at first this soon goes with practice.
Centre: Practising the herringbone.
Bottom: There is no shame in falling, it can be fun.**

BASIC SKILLS: POSTURE

How you stand on skis decides your rate of progress. You have to be able to stand comfortably and well balanced before thinking about controlling speed and turning, or coming down the fall line.

You'll hear a lot about the fall line. Where is it? It's the steepest line down from wherever you happen to be standing.

In our film we released a lot of coloured balls at the top of a hill. They were pulled by gravity down the line of least resistance.

That's what happens to you when you ski the fall line. And that is the real magic moment in ski-ing.

When you go down the fall line without turning, it's called straight running. Everybody finds it thrilling – and disconcerting.

I practised the correct posture with the TV five but with all of them there was in the upper body and arms a tenseness, as if they were trying to hang on to something.

If we could have seen inside anyone's boot we'd have found, I'm sure, that the toes were curled up trying to grip the skis. That is all very natural and you have to try to make yourselves aware of how every part of the body is reacting to this unique experience.

It is possible to condition yourself for this analysis. Do it before you ski by sensing what you are doing as you walk down the street, run, cycle, stand up, sit down.

Feel where the pressure is on the feet, how upright and straight or bent you are.

It sounds an odd thing to say but being aware just where your body is can be a great help in ski-ing, and indeed in all sports.

Test yourself
Study the picture taken of me (*right*) ski-ing down a glacier. What am I doing with my body? What's different?

The fall line, shown in blue throughout the book, is different for each of the three skiers.

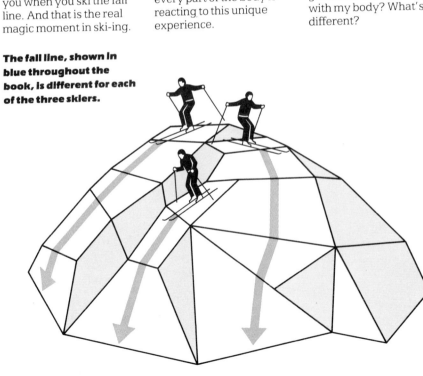

BASIC SKILLS: POSTURE

The human frame is not brilliantly designed for travelling at high speed over undulating terrain. For ski-ing we have to assume a posture that will feel quite abnormal at first. What does this mean in detail? You are bound to have noticed in the photograph on the preceding page that I am bent at the knees: I have turned my legs into shock absorbers or springs. I am flexed forward from the knees and from the ankles as well – a good boot allows me to bend forward from the ankles. What else? I have flexed the torso, bent forward from the waist – and pushed my pelvis forward. I have altogether lowered my centre of gravity. Try the posture now, standing up wherever you are.

Most teachers have their own comprehensive set of exercises to teach awareness of body position. I like the 1 to 10 Positions described at the foot of this page. Wearing boots if possible, practise assuming Position 6 in front of a mirror: there can be no substitute for self-awareness. Feedback from instructors and coaches is valuable, and you cannot learn to ski without this feedback from trained people in the early stages, but do try to develop a sense of where you are with hip, knee, ankle, torso. Practise standing still before you attempt to move.

Here are some points to watch:

1. Be careful when you bend at the waist that you don't produce a hollow back. The feeling should be of the hips being slightly tilted forward, as if you were sitting down on an invisible high stool Push forward from the pelvis.

2. Have you noticed a feeling that you are sitting back? The length of the thigh gives this feeling, but you may also be pushing yourself back. Don't. Stand up so that you've got the weight directly over your feet. When you have assumed Position 6 a few times, note where you feel pressure. You should feel it on the lower shin as the leg presses forward on the boot.

3. Female skiers shouldn't worry overmuch if they find it hard to copy my exact position. Females tend to be wider at the hips and to have knee joints that bend inwards slightly. If you're a woman, you're

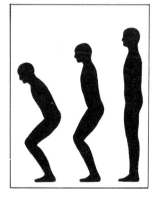

Above: Stretch as high as you can. Let's call that Position 1. Now go ten notches down as low as you can to Position 10. A good ski posture would be about 6.

Right: Note how I formed myself into an S.

exceptionally fit and supple if you can imitate my posture precisely.

Now you are ready to move. This exercise must be attempted on a slope where there is a run-out so that you don't have to think about stopping. We'll come to that – the first question every beginner asks is, 'When am I going to learn to stop?' Don't in any event try to stop by jamming the poles in front of you. You can easily run on to them with nasty consequences. Rather than do that, sit down to one side.

1. Stand with the skis apart, about hip-width. I don't care whoever shouts at you or how you feel. You must not deviate from this ski width in this practice at straight running – or the schuss, as it is commonly called. Don't attempt to keep the skis together. If you do, you will find you are not standing flat on the skis but on the outside edges; if you have your skis too far apart you are on the inside edges. Hip-width yields flat skis with a good chance of going straight down the fall line.

2. Stay on the flat at first, assume Position 6 and push off on the poles. Keep your hands in front with the ribs of the poles held loosely behind as in my example. The arms should stabilize you in the central

position as you move. It will take a little time to get used to this sliding feeling at low posture. Does it feel exaggerated? Good. That's how it should feel.

3. Move up the slope a little and try a longer slide. This is the time when there are a lot of falls. As you move a little faster you tend to sit back: the weight on the tails makes the skis shoot ahead of you and you fall backwards. Don't be depressed if you do this. When you lean forwards as a beginner, it is natural for you to fear you may plunge headlong over your ski tips. You won't. The boots and skis prop you up. As you realize this you will worry less and perform the proper forward flex. Think of trying to maintain your body at right angles to the slope at all times.

4. Cultivate an awareness of your feet. Are they relaxed or are your toes curled up tight? Have your toe nails gone through the boot soles? Have a word with them to relax. Think of standing *lightly* on a moving platform. Let the skis carry you down the slope – you

did intend to go down, didn't you?

5. It's natural to look at the skis as you move on them for the first time. It is not helpful. That is why awareness is so important: you should know where your skis are without having to look. When you look down you imperil your balance, if only

because you cannot be ready for little dips. This was one of the points brought out very well in the film, when Jon Lane gave us the view that most beginners have as they travel along looking down. It was quite frightening – much more frightening than taking your eyes off the skis. Look ahead the whole time.

My skis are hip-width apart, my arms helping me to keep my balance.

41

BASIC SKILLS: FEEL AND 'ELEGANCE'

'I can feel myself being tense because I'm not convinced it's a safe position yet,' said Jeremy. 'It just doesn't feel natural at the moment.' And Virginia: 'I see people ski-ing around who are not actually bending as much as we are being told to.'

Any other reactions would be surprising. It takes two or three days to begin to feel that the posture is right and easy. Of course, Virginia is right that you can see people who step off the lifts and seem to ski straight away in an upright posture. That's all right for experienced people on easy terrain, but it's no use for moving at speed or under stress. My aim with the group was to teach a basic posture which can be developed into other techniques, other movements.

And to create that all-important awareness. The first time anyone skis down a slope they concentrate not on a good ski posture but on staying upright – they are not aware of very much else. Only when you have done it a few times will you begin to relax enough to get into the right posture but even then it will feel strange for some time. Many resorts have video now and it is excellent to pay to have yourself filmed. Most people who do are astonished: they

'You cannot copy elegance. You can copy the movements and the positions which created that impression. But elegance can only come from having done something done well. You will never feel elegant at the moment or even good because all the positions are totally strange.'
ALI ROSS DURING FILMING

can remember doing some 'extreme' movement and when they see it on film it's not extreme at all; usually there hasn't been much adjustment on normal upright posture.

There must be constant effort at visualization. Watch film. Look at photographs. Dream ski-ing – I've dreamt ski-ing for many years. Avoid friends who already ski competently. I don't say this from the vested interest of a ski teacher, believe me. It's because over the years I have been asked to help out so many people who have been pushed to the brink of giving up by friends who have no idea any more of how awkward and how odd it feels for the beginner: they have forgotten what it was like and they no longer analyze themselves.

You will have many things said to you about your posture as you learn to ski, whether by those friends or teachers. Let's deal with some of them.

'That wasn't good.' Ignore it. The fact that you're sliding on skis at all is good enough for now. I prefer to say that at this stage you don't make mistakes, you make misunderstandings of what you see and hear.

'You're sitting back.' More helpful. What the speaker means to say is that you're not flexed forwards enough from the hip and knee. You are not really, as we say, standing on your feet. You resist doing this, as Jeremy indicated, from fear. Eliminate the fear by starting your straight running from lower down the slope. At this stage too much bravery can inhibit the learning process.

'Your bottom sticks out.' You may feel that yourself, but the simple fact of bending produces this sensation. What is worth attention is the *hollow back*. Keith had to master this problem, which was creating a lot of strain and stress for him.

I encouraged him to tilt his pelvis forward so that there was a better line through the spine and he was standing balanced over his feet. He found it strange to do at first.

You'll still be able to slide down a modest slope with a hollow back, but it is worth eliminating because it's not good posture and it will cause problems in the more advanced ski movements.

Exercise 1
Remember Positions 1 to 10? When you are confident in the straight running posture at Position 6, move up the slope a little and go for a longer slide where you move from Position 6 to Position 10 and then rise gently to 1 and back again to 6. It's an

'I'm very much aware of how I look. It's a shame that you have to lean forward and stick your bum out, because it doesn't look terribly good, I'm afraid. You're kitted out in this fantastic gear and you're very conscious of not quite living up to your costume'
JUNRI IN TV FILM

Note the S curve of his back — and the hollow in the lower spine of Junri,

exercise in which the normal Position 6 should be the central pivot.

Exercise 2
Again, only to be attempted when you are relaxed and comfortable in the basic posture, and *not* to be done at any real speed. Just before you come to a stop at the bottom of the slope, try changing direction by lifting one ski after another and stepping round. You will not turn like this as a rule but it is a very good balancing exercise.

Posture summary
Skis hip-width and flat for straight running. Flex at the ankles, flex at the knees, flex at the torso. Push the knees forward along the length of the skis. Tilt the pelvis forward to avoid a hollow back. Keep your eyes looking ahead.

Rate of progress
You should feel happy if at the end of two days you are able to:
● Carry skis properly and put them on unaided.
● Walk around and change direction on the flat.
● Slide down a short slope.
● Sidestep back up the hill.
We had achieved this at the end of four strenuous hours in our TV film with five fit people but, as I have said, two concentrated hours a day is enough for most people at the beginning.

BASIC SKILLS: CONTROL/FALLING/GETTING UP

We have climbed a slope. Now we want to come down it. I'll deal with the basic posture for that in the next few pages, but first you have to be able to position yourself for a short run down the slope — straight running, which means a slide without a turn.

I assume you have climbed twenty yards up a slope using the sidestep.
1. Stand across the fall line on your uphill edges. In this position the skis will not slip down the hill.
2. Don't move the skis, but swivel your upper body round so that you can reach down the slope with the poles. Stretch out with arms straight and plant both poles downhill about body-width apart.
3. Change your grip on the poles so that the tops butt into your palms. You'll need this for support in the next movement.
4. In small steps, move your skis round so that they face downhill. Lean on the poles to stop yourself sliding downhill.

There will be quite a lot of pressure on your arms at this stage.
5. Keep the skis flat, hip-width apart and pointing between your poles.
6. Raise poles for take-off. Assume basic posture (page 40) and slide between the poles. As you do, revert to your normal pole-grip.

Falling

I like to get people to take a tumble, especially in soft snow, to realize that there's nothing to it. On a steeper slope, remember this consoling thought: the snow is nearer to you! But there are right and wrong ways to fall. Bottoms were made for falling on, hands and knees were not, so if you feel you're about to fall, try to sit sideways into the slope. Keep your knees from the point of impact. Try to avoid falling forwards.

Getting Up

The first thing to do is nothing. It's an old law I see broken every day. Harold Evans has one of the earliest ski-teaching books, written in 1912 by Vivian Caulfield. Its theories are overtaken now but not her injunction: 'Never hurry, or try to struggle frantically to your feet without definite method.' Here's my definite method:

1. Check that you are in order, i.e. all your bits and pieces like feet, legs, skis, goggles, hat.

2. Look at the slope to judge the gradient.

Everyone falls over so it is important to learn the correct way to get up again.

3. Sit up. Assuming skis are still on, swing them around the slope and below you, so that they are across the fall line. Bend knees and bring the skis up as close to the chest as you can.

4. Take both poles, place the baskets behind you, perhaps a metre 2ft below the skis which are below you. Put the downhill hand, palm down, repeat palm down, at the foot of the poles. Put the uphill hand on top of the butts.

5. With pressure from the uphill one slide the downhill hand up the pole — and you get up with it.

6. Keep your uphill edges digging into the side of the hill so that you don't slip.

Getting up. How to 'walk' your hands up the sticks. Note how the skis are on their uphill edges, with knees into the hill.

Getting up with the hand acting as the escalator on the shafts of the poles is awkward at first attempt. Beginners forget to put the palm down, and they don't move the downhill hand quickly enough up the pole. But it comes. Some people stand up simply by putting both poles behind them. I think the method I have described is surer and safer, though sometimes *in deep snow* the baskets sink. You must then place the poles flat on the snow to form a cross and get up by placing your hand at its junction where it will not sink.

Sometimes one or both skis come off. Stand up. Have both skis side by side across the fall line. Remove snow from your boots. Plant the poles below the downhill ski, edge knee and ski into the hill and step into the binding, downhill ski first if both have come off.

CONTROL ON THE MOUNTAIN

To enjoy the rich gift of gravity skiers must learn control. There's no key to switch off the motor: ski-ing is not a stop-go sport.

For beginners there is no 'dead stop' which they can learn at once. The principal forms of control are to reduce speed by movement of the skis while maintaining the line of travel; to turn away from danger; and to turn uphill so that speed is reduced and motion then killed.

The faculty which must inform us of everything is perception. We must anticipate difficulties so that we can take action in plenty of time. We do that, of course, in driving a car, but ski-ing requires a heightened sense of anticipation and imagination because the environment is much more unpredictable, so are the other people, and there are no automatic aids.

Yet such is the thrill of speed and motion that even beginners allow themselves to ski out of control again and again. After a couple of days Jeremy and Virginia felt frustrated. They were doing well. They had tasted the pleasure of gravitational pull and they wanted more. They took off outside a restaurant and when I caught up with them the following conversation occurred:

Ali: 'What were you thinking about when you took off?'

Jeremy: 'Well, it's the first opportunity we've had to ski down from that particular point and I really think I was making the most of it.'

Virginia: 'The long quiet slope just seemed irresistible.'

Ali: I understand, but did you know you were really moving? You were doing about 25 miles an hour. Very fast, an incredible achievement for the short time you've been on skis. But wrong, because you were out of control. If there had been a child lying in the snow, as there sometimes is on that slope, you would have gone straight into him with these sharp skis. There's nothing you could have done about it.'

Jeremy: 'Well, that speed sounds exaggerated to me, but your criticism is probably fair.'

The Learning Curve

This is a difficulty for a teacher. I didn't want to dampen their marvellous enthusiasm, yet control is vital for everyone's safety and enjoyment. And it's also my conviction that haste at this stage is in fact counter-productive. The learning achievement curve is steeper if we master the basic movements on the nursery slopes and always ski in control.

I believe in spending at least three days doing this. Beginners who rush early on often fall to pieces when confronted with difficult terrain because they haven't built a solid basis. They have probably managed on muscle power rather than on ski power.

Secondly, I believe that intermediates who reach a plateau do so because they have spent insufficient time on the basics.

I understand that everyone enjoys a sense of progress and that they feel this is marked by tackling more and more dramatic slopes. But I'm sure it is more constructive to ski down a manageable slope several times a day effectively at a nice speed and enjoying it, than to push yourself to a point where you struggle, fall, and generally terrify yourself by taking on too much. This puts you mentally back at the second day and it takes extra time to restore the confidence gained during the first three or four days.

Gain understanding. You can get by on a modest slope and at reasonable speed with an imperfect understanding of what you are doing. But the cracks show when you are under pressure later. So I come back to my constant theme: no matter who the teacher is, there's only one person who can do the learning, and that's you.

CONTROL: GLIDING AND BRAKING SNOW PLOUGH

How do I stop?' Beginners ask the question even before they've moved. At this stage we never learn how to stop dead – that's quite a strenuous process. What we must learn is control. That we can acquire, and it is fundamental to all you do in ski-ing. Control is a better concept for us than stopping or even slowing down: these get in the way of the learning process. After all, ski-ing is about moving and controlling that movement. However, it's impossible to expect anyone to think anything except stopping if they learn on a steepish slope. That's why it is so important to spend these early days on a slope which is friendly – one for which you almost have contempt.

The first means of control is called the wedge or snow plough. The name suggests what it is: you put the skis in a V-position, tips together, heels apart. There is a gliding snow plough, which I am doing on this page, and a braking snow plough, which is on the facing page. Pause for a moment and see if you can analyze the movements.

1. I assume the normal hip-width running posture, with skis flat, knees bent, pelvis forward, hands forward, tips of poles to the rear – about Position 5.

2. I let the skis slide for a

few yards. As I come down the slope, I gently but positively push my feet equally apart.

3. The knees stay forward. Note the arrows on my trousers – we designed those to make everything clearer on the TV film. I haven't twisted my knees round at all: they are pressing forward along the line of the skis. This means my feet have formed a V in line with my skis.

4. What has happened to my skis? They have been put lightly on their inner edges.

5. The more I push feet and legs apart, the more my skis are edged. It's automatic.

6. The wider the V, the greater *the braking area* of ski on snow. There is a physical limit to how far I can press out but on a reasonable slope I would have a V wide enough to provide a sufficient braking area to bring me slowly to a stop. But I am not trying to stop.

That fact is so important that I'm going to repeat it many times, I am not trying to stop. As soon as beginners think of the snow plough as a way of stopping, instead of letting the skis act naturally in their own time, they try to force themselves to stop. Body posture is lost. Everything goes wrong.

CONTROL: THE PLOUGH IN PRACTICE

The movement

Do 'the splits' a few times. I asked the TV beginners when they were standing still on the flat to forget their skis — just open the legs and rotate the feet inwards.

Of course they had skis on and when they did the splits in this way their skis opened with the tips together and the heels apart.

I just wanted them to get used to the idea of leg movement and foot rotation; and the movement nicely stretched their tendons and muscles.

Beginners always used to be told to push the heels of the skis apart. That is a mistaken instruction for two reasons.

First, it makes them think about forcing the skis to do something — and sudden, excess physical effort has bad consequences on posture.

Second, talking about the heels of the skis takes the mind backwards to the rear of the body. When beginners do the snow plough thinking about the heels of the skis, they tend to sit back too much.

The posture

The normal straight running posture feels low. If we increase the distance between our feet, we decrease body height and feel even lower. If you think of the gliding plough

as Position 5 on our ten-point scale, think of the wide, braking plough as Position 4 on the scale.

Your first attempt

Do 20 movements on the flat before attempting the gliding plough on a friendly slope.

Then let the skis run and near the bottom, softly and slowly slide the feet apart a little, rotate the feet and hold the V-position.

When you are happy with this, start the gliding plough at the top. Position yourself, using the poles as I have described on page **40**, so that you start off dead central, standing with your weight evenly on both skis.

Halfway down push out more into the braking plough, keeping yourself (and the skis) divided by an imaginary central line.

Fears, problems and illusions

When we tried it for the TV film, this is what happened: everyone

veered to one side or the other because they didn't stand evenly between the skis or because they threw themselves off-centre by excess movement.

Junri didn't lower her body posture; she was stiff-legged.

Virginia tried to stop, with the result that she threw her arms about and lost symmetry.

Keith and Melanie sat back stiff-legged. Keith tried to force his skis apart.

Jeremy tried to force his knees together.

Two optical illusions were manifest.

'I was trying to bend the knees forward and together like you,' said Jeremy.

But I never try to bring the knees together in a plough: I press forward, to make my knees follow the length of the skis. Because the tips are together the knees *appear* to be moving together, but I am not trying to produce that effect. It is a consequence, not a cause.

And trying to move the knees together is likely to put one ski or the other on edge too much (which, in turn, produces a wing to one side or the other when you are trying to go straight).

The second optical illusion is of sitting back.

When I came to a stop in the braking plough I might have *appeared* to sit back; if I did, it was in reality a fractional compensation for the stop effect.

Knees must be bent and pushed forward along the skis. Sitting back is excess prudence: the typical beginner feels safer the more he removes himself from his speeding tips.

We had tried the braking and gliding plough by the end of our second day. Everyone gained in confidence; Virginia and Jeremy, in particular, wanted to go faster.

I was a bit of a spoilsport, insisting on straight, absolutely controlled snowploughing before we moved on.

When both legs are parallel the skis are flat. When we open them out the skis are edged automatically.

The group practise first stationary until the position feels less strange.

Keith's tenseness is obvious.

Junri in a good well-balanced plough glide.

TURNING: FEEL THE FORCES

You do not have to be an acrobat to be a skier. Any physically normal person can assume a technically correct ski-ing position. We do it every day. When the Underground train brakes with people standing, their reaction is a defensive hip-lean. I was explaining this point one day to Graham Davis, the designer of our book. 'You can get into as good a ski-ing position as I can,' I told him. He was incredulous. The main photograph on this page is the result of an experiment we undertook to settle the argument.

Graham Davis has never been on skis in his life. I gave him no instruction. I told him simply to arrange

to have himself photographed standing on a flat trailer being pulled at speed in circles. I was not even there when he made the experiment.

And the result is Graham Davis in a technically perfect turning position. Once he had got used to the car driver stopping and starting, Graham never fell over sideways once. He adjusted his leg lean and hip position to compensate for the pull to the outside of the turn.

The skateboarder and roller skaters do just the same thing (bottom left) without any instruction or training. So do the bowler hats on the tube. The position is one in which the

knees are pressing forward, with ankles bent. The leg leans inwards, taking the hips inwards. The arms are forwards and outwards, providing stabilization for the upper body.

Could Graham do this on skis? Yes, he could. Why then cannot everyone ski at once, without instruction? My theory is that the difference between trailer riding/ skateboarding/tube riding etc and ski-ing is that in the first group of movements there is friction, therefore the body receives positive feedback and adjusts

naturally to the forces it can sense. But on skis we have a sliding base and the feedback is not so positive, therefore everyone feels insecure. Fear produces defensive movements which happen to be the reverse of what is required and of what would occur naturally.

To learn ski-ing, we have to improve the

To photograph good ski-ing positions, I took my camera to the National Film Theatre in London where the skateboarders practise. Like Graham on the moving trailer, this youth is in a sound position for turning at speed on snow.

feedback from the ski. If there is one secret of good ski-ing it is this: learn to use the edges of the skis and the feedback becomes much more positive.

There is a more basic appreciation which can make an enormous difference to learning. It is that ski-ing is a dynamic sport. That sounds obvious. But when we look at a skier we tend to freeze his position in the mind, very much as a still photographer can freeze a moment at speed. It's easier to recall a still image than a moving one, therefore we programme ourselves to reproduce in our own ski-ing a static image.

But what we have seen and remembered has been created by dynamic movements in a dynamic situation. To reproduce it we have to know and understand how it was created in the first place. I feel strongly that people do not make mistakes. They make misunderstandings.

TURNING: UNDERSTANDING WHAT HAPPENS

It is not possible to learn to sail effectively unless we can imagine and then understand the effect of the wind on the sail or on the boat: The wind is the energy and the force we have to understand. In ski-ing that force is gravity, the force that pulls us down the hill.

If ski-ing were just going straight downhill, as the speed trialists do, it would be a relatively simple matter of having the courage and the skills to stand on skis going in one direction. But recreational ski-ing is about controlled turning, which allows us to go where we want at the speed we can manage. When we start to move on skis we develop momentum; therefore we have to understand what

happens when the direction of that momentum is changed: a force is created. Think of it very simply like this: any heavy object travelling at speed in a curve will be subjected to a pull *to the outside of that curve*.

Knowing this is crucial to making sense of the instructional phrases and commands in conventional ski instruction. Taken at face value, for instance, the instruction to shift weight to the outside ski can be misleading – it does not produce the right body position to create a good turn and can produce a very bad one. It also obscures the fact that it is the force to the outside of the turn which is responsible for the distribution of weight. If,

on the other hand, the skier understands that he has to resist the force, he is much more likely to position his centre of mass (i.e. hips) to the centre of the turn – the perfect ski-ing position.

On a pair of skis relatively small movements of the body can produce dramatic effects – far more dramatic

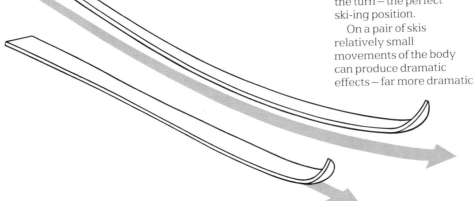

Moving the leg and knee inwards puts pressure on the ski's edge and because of its shape and design this makes the ski bend. The degree of pressure and edging dictates the degree of bend. The turn is created by the bending and will be a wide or a sharp turn according to how little or how much pressure is put on the edge. Melanie is practising the knee/leg movement on the flat.

in fact than violent movements which are made without any understanding of what is happening. The less skilful skier, throwing himself about the slope, always feels that he is having trouble with his skis: to him – or her! – they are clumsy and hard to turn. So they are if the skier relies only on muscles to do the turning. Add to this the physical insecurity of a sliding, skidding base and it's a wonder anyone enjoys the sport at all.

The faster we go the stronger is the pull and a good skier uses that pull wisely, able to marry perception of the forces at work with a knowledge of how the ski is designed to exploit them.

What the Ski Will Do

There is no need for me to attempt a long analysis of the physical properties of the ski. All we need to appreciate is that it is a turning machine. The tip of the ski is wide, the middle or the waist is narrow, and the heel is wide again. When the ski is put on its edge and pressured, it bends into an arc. The radius of the arc depends on the degree of edge and the degree of pressure. The radius of the arc determines the radius of our turns.

I carry on to the slopes a small piece of cardboard to illustrate this point. It's only a very simplified description of a ski – which has other properties such as camber, flex pattern and torsional rigidity – but I've found that that bit of cardboard and a knowledge of the forces at work on the skier have helped many people to help themselves off the plateau.

Carving and Skidding

Ten years ago the vocabulary of ski-ing did not include the word carving. When the three authors introduced it into the original *We Learned to Ski* they described it as the action of the skier simply riding round the radius of the turn, his edges locked into an arc like a tram on a curving monorail. In short, the perfect exploitation of the turning properties of the ski **with no skid**. The track of the carved turn is a simple groove in the snow; the track of the skidded turn is a broader arc.

This is a valuable concept – but it's important not to be intimidated by it, not to allow an idea of the perfect carved turn to get in the way of our progress by making us believe that any degree of skid is wrong. Skidders can be carvers and carvers can skid. I believe that even the most perfect carved turn has an element of skid in it. This is another example of the way ski terminology produces barriers, just as 'parallel' produces inhibitions and 'style' can get in the way of more efficient ski-ing.

There are two kinds of skid. Some people skid a lot because they make mistakes, because they're not adjusting their bodies to the forces. But there are skiers with good basic technique who skid a good controlled curve. They are not carvers simply because they have not yet developed the awareness and sensitivity necessary for that but they are effective skiers.

Skidding is a necessary part of our repertoire which will enable us to cope with any conditions on the mountain. Carving is a necessary technique for the racer and an aspiration for the recreational skier.

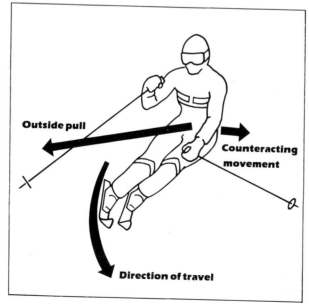

Outside pull

Counteracting movement

Direction of travel

To put things simply, any heavy object travelling at speed in an arc will be subjected to a pull to the outside of the arc. In ski-ing this means that the outside or downhill pull is responsible for weight distribution, not any action on our part and to counteract this force we must set the hips – our centre of mass – away from the pull.

TURNING: BASIC SNOW PLOUGH

Ski-ing is turning, but when you start to learn to turn the idea of turning is itself unhelpful. Walking down the street we can change direction in a flash with a pivot on the heel. We have to shed the notion that turning on skis is anything like that. The ski has to turn along an arc. That requires us to be patient. The more we want to turn, the more difficult it may be for us to learn unless we adapt to this different method in a different environment. A series of exercises helps.

1. Find a long but gentle slope.

2. Glide down it for a little way in the plough, then push the feet out and sink into the braking plough.

3. Now rise into the faster gliding plough. After a short way once again sink back into the braking plough.

4. Do this several times, aiming for a smooth rhythmic movement down the fall line. Feel the difference between the braking and gliding plough.

Your feet change direction in this exercise, and so do your skis, but so far the skis have not changed your direction. Now you will do that. Choose a big broad slope with few people around.

1. Begin with the same rhythmic gliding/braking

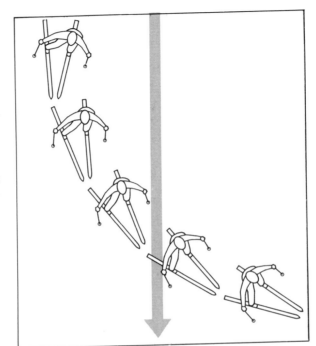

movement down the slope, but now simply try it *on one leg*. Don't try to turn. Just push the foot out on one side for a gliding plough. If you do find yourself turning slowly across the fall line, that's fine. But no effort at turning, please.

2. Try it with the other leg.

3. Try again, but this time try to put two one-leg braking ploughs into the run.

4. Rise up into the gliding plough after each one. It will take time for the skis to drift back into the fall line. Wait for that. Then let the skis run a little before doing the braking movement again.

These movements will produce a simple, light change of direction. Don't go too far out of the fall line.

What we are practising here is a half-turn. Don't try to cram in too many per run. Two good half-turns are better than a botched half-dozen.

One thing I can't emphasize enough when you're doing these exercises – or any movements – on the slopes is that you must forget how you look to other people. Self-awareness is what you're aiming for, and everyone else is pretty busy with their own ski-ing anyway. Make sure, though, that you don't cut anyone up in your concentration. Look before you move.

TURNING: THE KNEE EXERCISE IN THE PLOUGH

I gave the TV group a number of exercises which anyone can try. My basic aim was to get them to feel the skis moving underneath them in the same way as the skis would move in a turn – but I never mentioned the words 'turn' or 'weight' to our group. I wanted them never to acquire those habits that you see on all the ski slopes, of people rotating their shoulders and generally flinging themselves around to move their weight and get the skis to turn. Once you are in a good plough position, no physical effort is needed to hold the skis there. On very steep slopes there is a certain amount of physical effort, but basically it is the same throughout ski-ing: it is the way we set our skis that controls our speed, not physical input.

Two exercises will help you to realize this:
1. Come down the slope in a glide plough. Roll your knees from side and feel the degree to which the skis are edged.
2. Glide the whole way down the slope, but near the bottom progressively move one knee forwards and inwards. This brings the ski over on its edge, and allows the ski to take you round the corner.

This next exercise can be performed very effectively by leaning down and putting a hand on a knee, as I am doing in the picture. Do it to one side only at first.

Linking Turns
1. As soon as you feel a change of direction, across the fall line, remove your hand and come back to base, that is, rise into the gliding plough. Take time to come into the fall line again. Relax.
2. Hand on knee again. Press inward. Wait for the reaction. Repeat exercise. At this stage take care that the whole leg leans inward and not only the knee.

What you are doing here, of course, is putting the ski on edge. When you feel balanced and comfortable, try pressurizing the other knee, pushing it gently inwards with your hand. Again, come back to base as soon as you feel a change of direction, and glide down the fall line. You will need some momentum. If you go too slowly, you will not change direction.

The Common Faults
How did our guinea pigs fare? That's a good guide to how most people will respond.

Too rushed
I found myself calling to everyone, 'Let them run.'

Melanie, Jeremy and Keith went too quickly from pressing the knee one way to pressing it the other. There must be a distinct gap between one change of direction and another. Return to the glide, relax as the skis go down the fall line, gather speed, and then press in on one knee.

Too slow
Junri, on the other hand, spent too long with her hand pressing on the knee. What happened? 'I turned round so much I thought I was going back up the slope again!' She had by accident performed the right movement for stopping, which is to turn the skis uphill, but the wrong movement for ski-ing down the slope. Also, Junri started off across the fall line instead of coming straight down it, so she had not enough speed for the exercise to work.

Awkwardness
'I found it very hard to organize myself to push the knee inwards,' said Virginia. 'I felt I wanted to push it out and that's not what's required, presumably. It seems unnatural.' It well might, I told Virginia. Every new step we try in ski-ing feels strange because it is new. That does not mean it is wrong.

Excessive edge
Melanie traced off the slope in a sharp unbalanced turn because she had excessive edge. Why? Because she was already in a wide plough when she pushed in with the knee. The movement is made from a narrow gliding plough. The skis must be skidding before the turning pressure is applied by pressing the knee inwards.

Not enough forethought
'I went to pieces. I was thinking too much,' said Keith. 'By the time I had worked it out, I was at the bottom of the slope.'

Keith was not alone in setting off without having decided what he was going to do; Virginia did the same. It's partly from trying too hard for success. I told them: 'I want you to forget about succeeding. Just decide you are going to make these movements and wait and see what happens.'

Moving weight
I spotted Jeremy moving his weight across from one ski to the other. It led to the ski being flattened, rather than edged.

'Transfer your weight' and 'Lean out' are common instructions I prefer to avoid because I find they can easily be misinterpreted by beginners. They think of making flat movements the only way they know how, as they might in walking, just shifting pressure from one foot to the other. Instead, think of the positions and movements which create weight distribution.

TURNING: LINKING THE PLOUGHS

My next step was to get the five to link the plough turns, and gradually to assume the correct position without reaching down to touch the knee. We think of three stages:

1. Neutral position, which is gliding down the fall line.

2. Turning position, in which the knee and leg go in, lowering body position.

3. Neutral position again as soon as the deflection of direction has occurred.

So we glide, curve, glide. Curving or turning is a lower position, so we are down; gliding is a higher position, so we are up. But simply to interpret these movements as 'up' and 'down' leads to errors. As I reminded Junri, it's important to understand what creates our decrease in height, and what creates our increase in height. She started to interpret 'down' as a simple sitting-down movement – which it is not. That produces a hollow back. The basic S-posture must be maintained, and the impression of a down movement must be created only by the lean inwards of knee, leg and hip.

The same point applies to pressure differences. Keith remarked that he had been 'concentrating on transferring his weight', which is revealing because I never mention weight transfer: it

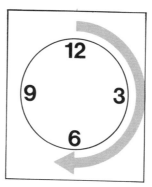

Think of the face of a clock. The beginning of the turn is around twelve o'clock and the end at six o'clock. There's a different body position or an increased movement for each hour to six o'clock. So we don't really stop moving from the time we start to turn to the time the turn is finished. If we have to turn quicker, we still must go through each 'hour'.

misleads the learner. The ski on the outside of the curve will have more pressure on it than the ski on the inside – but we shouldn't think of that as the prime object. If we do think of the movement as a shift of weight we invariably make one which flattens the ski and then it's useless for turning.

In addition to these misunderstandings there was simple fear of the fall line, so that one or the other would attempt to turn by screwing the skis round, rotating hip and shoulders, instead of letting the ski describe an arc.

The Run to Brandegg

At this stage, I decided the group was ready for a run. Melanie and Junri had had a grumble about the pace. Everyone was nicely frustrated by three days of practice! It's four miles from the railway station to the station and café at Brandegg. It's basically a wood path, never particularly steep anywhere, and marked blue.

Having learned good basic techniques our five were all visibly improving their turns as they made one after another on the long run. At the end, the skis of Junri, Virginia and Jeremy were coming closer together in the plough turn and glide, and occasionally, though they didn't know it, they were making parallel turns.

'Wonderful, lovely, I begin to understand what ski-ing is all about,' said Junri. 'Exhilarating, it all came together somehow,' said Jeremy. 'Anyone who says he wasn't frightened once or twice,' said Keith, 'must be absolutely fearless, but it was fantastic.' He sniffed the mountain air with satisfaction: 'It's boosted my confidence no end.' So it had.

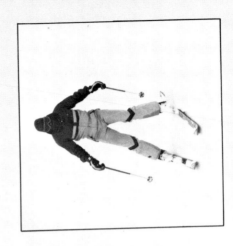

Rising into a shallow gliding plough to the fall line. This is where I change the edge of my new turning ski.

THE EVOLUTION OF THE TURN

Here in one run down a slope at Wengen is a demonstration of the truth that the positions and movements learned in our very basic plough turn are the same positions and movements used by advanced skiers who ski parallel. At the top I am going slowly, making plough turns. As I allow the skis to run and speed up, the plough becomes narrower and towards the end of the turns the skis are skidding closer together. In my last two turns here the skis have become parallel – without any change in my basic position.

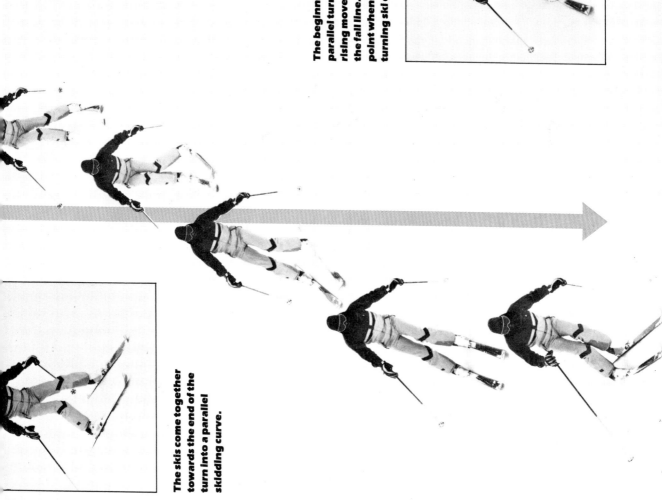

The beginning of the parallel turn. A committed rising movement towards the fall line. This is the point when I put my new turning ski on edge.

The skis come together towards the end of the turn into a parallel skidding curve.

ON THE MOVE: THE TRAVERSE

There were a couple of slopes on the blue run to Brandegg that were too steep for the group to ski down. We traversed, which means we skied across the face of the slope. The traverse cuts speed, by comparison with the schuss. How much slower you go depends on the angle of the traverse. If you ski down, say, at twenty-five minutes past five it is almost as fast as ski-ing down in a six o'clock schuss.

The choice of angle depends on your objective. A traverse is useful for covering distance without losing height. Sometimes you want to do that on a long journey: the traverse opens up the mountain. By putting together a long traverse and a turn at the end it's possible to travel over wide and quite difficult areas.

I had not taught the five the traverse when we did our run, but the ingredients were there. The profile of the body in the plough is the same as when traversing, except that in the traverse the skis are parallel.

Posture practice

1. With skis at right-angles to the fall line, reach down and outwards with your pole to touch the lower slope a yard or two from your position. Or stand up in the living-room, if you like, and do it with a walking stick.

2. You will feel pressure on your downhill ski (or outside foot). It is a natural consequence of your movement. Remember that. It's the same pressure you felt when bending the leg inwards to make a plough turn. It's very similar also to sidestepping up the hill. The steeper the hill, the more pressure you feel, and the more the ski is edged to prevent you sliding.

3. What has happened to the rest of the body?

Knees, hip, shoulders: all tilt in at the same angle. The upper body and upper ski lead slightly – you'll find it hard otherwise to make the necessary inward push of the knees and hips which produces the required edging. And if the uphill ski is ahead it will not cross.

The position comes naturally enough off skis. Walk across a steep slope or concrete ramp and you'll see. We go into the traverse position without any instruction at all, because we feel the pull of gravity and resist it. But when we ski across in a traverse we are on a sliding base.

Compare the plough position (far left) and the traverse. The ski is open in the plough but lines drawn from plough shoulder to traverse shoulder, hip to hip, leg to leg, would be parallel.

Ski tips will not cross when the upper ski is ahead. I have my knees together but the skis a little apart.

ON THE MOVE: THE BEGINNERS TRAVERSE

Left: The static skier easily assumes the right position in response to my pull.

Above: It's helpful to the idea of maintaining hip, leg and knees in position to ski a shallow traverse this way.

Everyone who tries the traverse first time feels its awkward posture. Yet if I imitate gravity with beginners they always immediately assume the perfect ski-ing position (see above) without a word of advice.

'Give me your hand,' I say, 'and I'll try to pull you down the slope.' I pull gently but firmly and the skier adopts the position above. Note the edging of the skis.

This is what happened when we tried it moving:

Keith hung back. The knees go into the mountain but we still need them pushed forward as in the basic posture. Feel the pressure on the shinbone.

Junri and Virginia pushed their knees in all right, but more is required: the whole leg must go in sideways, producing angulation. If we push only the knees in, the hip rotates and the upper body faces uphill. I could see them forcing their shoulders round to compensate for the displaced hip. The same fault occurs from thinking of putting weight on the downhill ski. We're looking for *lateral* movement of the legs. This will produce angulation, increased or decreased edging of the ski and proper weight distribution.

Melanie had her feet too wide apart. Hip-width, no more, is right for proper angulation.

Start right, end right. One of the most learned people in British, if not European, ski-ing is John Sheddon and he stresses: 'Think before you move. Think about what you want to do and then simply do it.' I know from my experience how often people move off with only the vaguest idea of what they intend to do.

Set yourself up for a traverse and before moving off check:
- top half of the body is ahead
- knees and legs are into the slope holding the skis on their edges
- pressure is felt on the front of the boot
- poles are apart and forward for balance, tips trailing

It feels exaggerated but try to relax so that one part of the body is not fighting another.

Play around on a gentle slope. Keith (foreground) is practising the traverse exercise of stretching out with the ski stick. But his heart's not in it. Compare the inadequate angulation with the Isaac Newton effect (left).

ON THE MOVE: SIDESLIP

The group soon learned to sideslip and, added to the traverse, it meant there was almost nowhere on the piste they couldn't go. From now on they free-skied quite a lot.

With the sideslip you can lose height without gaining speed, so you can come down a steep slope without having to try a turn. You can ski across a slope with a mix of traverse and moving sideslip. The sideslip was important to the group for another reason: as they went faster their skis gradually came together, so that they were turning or skidding sideways with their skis parallel.

Like most ski movements, the sideslip generates misconception. As I told the group: 'When you saw me slide sideways down that slope, it was natural to think it was some effort of mine that was making the skis slip. It wasn't. Gravity pulls us down the slope. We've just learned to hold those skis on their edges in the traverse to stop gravity pulling us down. What we do in the sideslip is simply to say, all right, I give in. Pull me.'

The sideslip is based on the traverse. As we cross the slope we reverse the position of the knees and legs: instead of leaning them into the hill, we lean them downhill. This flattens the skis and we

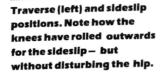

Traverse (left) and sideslip positions. Note how the knees have rolled outwards for the sideslip — but without disturbing the hip.

slip. That's all there is to it. When we want to stop, we resume the traverse position – knees and legs leaning inwards – which resets the uphill edges.

Try it on a fairly steep slope or the pull of gravity won't be enough, and you're likely to push with your hips and catch an edge. The steeper the slope the easier it is to sideslip. As we slip

downhill, we look downhill a little more: after all, that's the direction we are now going.

The main trouble for the group was moving the hip out, trying to force the skis to slide. This leads to the downhill edge catching and a fall, or the uphill ski may be left stranded. Awkward. Roll the knees evenly but keep hips in the traverse position.

Direction is a product of posture. If the tips swing uphill and the tails down, you're sitting back. Experiment with fore and aft balance.

The forward sideslip. We need speed to maintain forward downward slide. Note how the hips and body face direction of travel.

BUILDING ON THE PLOUGH TURN

The parallel turn evolves by building on the plough turn.

I encouraged my group to go faster and faster in the plough without any emphasis on the relationship of one ski to another.

Here is what happens in a speeded-up plough turn. As I come through the fall line in the plough, my speed is such that the pressure on the outside ski is greatly increased. This means that there is less pressure on my inside ski. It drifts naturally towards the turning ski, so that at the end my skis are parallel. I must emphasize: I am not trying at this stage to make my skis parallel. It

A midway stage in the evolution from the plough to the parallel is the basic swing. It's the first turn from traverse to traverse (linked plough turns are down a gentle fall line, repeat gentle).

THE BASIC SWING

The turn starts with a *narrow*, gliding plough and uses exactly the same movements and positions as the plough turn. But the speed is greater than in the plough and if we resist the pull to the outside of the turn by progressively leaning the leg to the centre of the turn, the skis

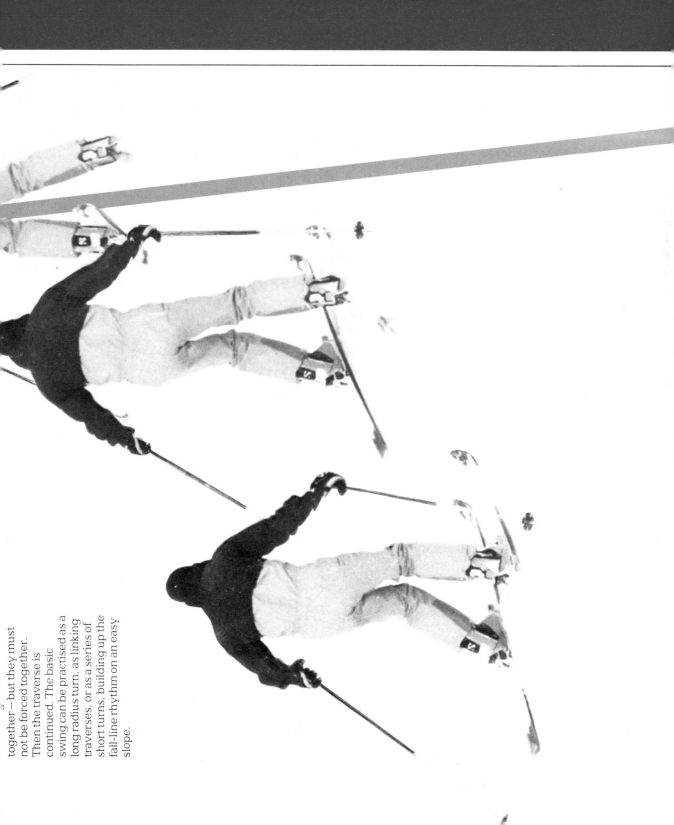

together – but they must not be forced together. Then the traverse is continued. The basic swing can be practised as a long radius turn, as linking traverses, or as a series of short turns, building up the fall-line rhythm on an easy slope.

THE PLOUGH AND THE ADVANCED TURN COMPARED

I often think that the people who gave the fashionable cachet to 'parallel ski-ing' created a monster. Everyone wants to ski parallel because they see it as the stylish and right thing to do. This leads to all sorts of learning problems. One of the reasons so many thousands of intermediates get stuck on a plateau is that they misinterpret what they see. It so happens that the best skiers do seem to have their skis in parallel — if not glued together! But never for a moment, in fact, does the good skier force the skis together.

Learn to love your plough turn! That's the message for every skier, because the basic movements and positions for the plough turn are the same as for the parallel turn. Here I am in the plough (far right) and in the parallel (near right) at the same stage of a turn. Note the common features:

- the inward lean of the turning leg, creating edge on the ski
- the angulation between the upper body and the leg
- the hips — centre of mass of the body — are to the centre of the turn, resisting the force trying to pull me sideways
- the forward thrust of the bent knees.

The only difference you

can see between these two turns is that in the near right turn, my skis are parallel. Why? Not because I forced them together, thinking I would ski parallel. The reason was that in the parallel turn I was going faster. The forces in the turn are therefore greater and it is these forces, basically, which help to produce the parallel effect.

Time taken to learn these movements and positions at the plough stage pays handsome dividends. Intermediate and advanced skiers should come back to the plough to train for more advanced techniques, such as carving. Warren Witherell in the United States, who has for years trained national racers, puts them back to doing plough turns to improve their basic techniques.

Melanie summed up my approach perfectly at the end of the filming: 'The idea that we were making parallel turns was only introduced when we achieved them. This was clever because if Ali had said categorically, 'Now, we are going to learn a new turn,' I for one would immediately have had a mental block and found the so-called new manoeuvre impossible for a while. As it was, the parallel turn was just a development of what we had already learned.'

FIVE WHO LEARNED TO SKI...

At the end of two weeks I was able to lead all five of our 'beginners' on any of the standard runs; they were no longer beginners. But it's best to let them sum up. First Keith, whose marvellous temperament helped him to overcome the disadvantages of height and weight. When he fell the mountain got the worst of it!

Keith: 'I couldn't get the braking plough to stop me on anything more than a very modest slope. That fact, plus not having any real control over my direction, did not inspire early confidence. I must admit I would have liked to have learned to stop dead (e.g. parallel christie stop) far earlier in the course, but I accept that it could have created more problems than it solved.

I liked the way the theory of turning was put across in such a simple way – knees flex, fall line, reach with the outer arm. It gave a couple of movements to concentrate on. It still sticks in my mind very clearly all these months later.

At times of panic it was tempting to use brute strength to make turns, but towards the end we had practised the correct way so much that this idea really was banished from my thoughts.

My lasting impression of learning to ski is that it was psychologically as well as physically very tiring, and was unlike any other learning curve.

The learning process takes you through a series of stable plateaux but in order to progress to the next point of stability, you have to enter the realms of instability, which can present a psychological barrier (e.g becoming competent at straight ploughs, then having to learn to turn in a plough).

'But, in summary, the regular goading to stretch ourselves alternated with the laborious attention to detail bore fruit in the incredible advances shown in the latter stages of the course. I can remember looking back in disbelief at some slopes that I had successfully manoeuvred.'

Virginia: 'I was 38, and this sounded an advanced age for learning. However, I was determined – perhaps too strongly – to put up at least as good a show as the younger students. I've always expected to master something new quickly and the patience needed to grasp each step was hard for me to muster. It became clear towards the end that those who had proceeded slowly and carefully at first were in the end doing better, simply because they'd taken the time.

'The most useful piece of advice? To lean *out*,

always. And perhaps the trick of imagining you are holding a hoop in front of you. But above all for me it was the often repeated: Think what you're going to do before you do it '

Melanie: 'The physical concentration, and sheer difficulty of training the body to execute moves which are not easy, plus altitude, cold, sun and bright light, make ski-ing a very demanding sport. At first my approach was negative and so my progress was equivalent. Later, when I began to see the effort as an exciting challenge, I felt I could relax about my physical inability to co-ordinate my moves, and as soon as I did the moves just came of their own accord. In fact, Ali had guided us into ski-ing by teaching us the basic discipline, and then allowing us to develop it from inside. Points I found helpful:

● Ali suggested that we should position our hips by imagining sitting on an invisible chair on the uphill side of the slope.

● I always remembered him saying that you cannot fall if you are moving forward. When turning into the fall line, I said to myself, you can't fall, you fool, you are still moving forwards . . . and by that time I had turned.

● Ski-ing very carefully the first few runs lays the foundation for the

rest of the day.

● Ali's explanation that the skis do the work. Skis bend and if the skier applies the correct pressure, then the ski turns without any weight redistribution, without twisting the body.

'The most enjoyable part for me was judging the terrain in advance and deciding how to negotiate it. For example, bumps. Ali said turn off the back of them. I tried it and it worked. It was also comforting to be able to traverse and sideslip.'

Jeremy: 'I enjoyed the learning process. I got a great kick out of doing terrain we hadn't covered before, unnerving but exciting. I found I didn't mind falling over. I enjoyed my runs, though I became a bit conscious of people burning down behind me . . . Next year that'll be me.'

Junri: 'At first I was afraid of falling and because I was afraid I'd do anything to avoid it and was getting terribly tense. But after a couple of falls you discover it doesn't hurt and in fact it's a sort of relief. The worst has happened so you can go on and try more things. I didn't realize my feelings could go up and down so much. But it's not true, in fact. I do go up and down elsewhere but it's only here I relate it to ski-ing.'

Melanie

Jeremy

Junri

Keith

Virginia

GETTING OFF THE PLATEAU

The five beginners had sweltered in the sun. When the four intermediates arrived the weather changed. They had blizzards, fog, complete white-outs where it was barely possible to see ten yards ahead, and days of winds which sliced through anoraks at the top of the mountain. And after all the earlier sun the snow was thinner on the lower slopes, exposing rock and root. Not ideal conditions for restoring confidence and getting off the plateau.

JANE

Jane broke her leg ski-ing when she was 19, nine years before this trip to Wengen. She had not had skis on since. When the accident happened she was working in a mountain restaurant and heading back to work after a pleasant morning. It was fairly flat where the tips of her skis touched rock. She somersaulted and the bindings did not release. 'Nobody came by. It was quite a nice sunny day. I just lay there and waited. It was just a case of bad equipment.' Jane had skied for seven winters (two weeks each time) from the age of 12, and had learned in Switzerland.

JIM AND COREY

We thought of them as a pair because they were both powerfully built men from the American Embassy in London. Jim, aged 30, had never had a lesson in his life. 'I think of myself as a lower intermediate. I get down the slopes eventually, maybe a spill or two here and there, but I get down in one piece. After two weeks of lessons, I expect to put the Maher brothers out of business.' Jim had not skied for five years.

Corey, aged 38, had skied more recently but had not had a lesson in ten years. 'I'm a bit ragged. I go down the slope but not with much aplomb.'

ELLY

Aged 30, had learned her ski-ing in Austria and had seven years' experience, two weeks at a time. She is adept at many sports — riding, cycling, running, swimming, water-ski-ing, and enjoys contemporary dance as well.

On the Mountain

Jane set everyone's mind at rest. 'Once I started to ski I just found there was no place in my tiny brain for worrying about the accident I had. I was very afraid before I started going down the slope, but once I got goint it was fantastic.'

Ali Ross watched them all ski and commented: 'As I expected, it's essential to take everyone back to the very, very beginning and treat them the same way as I treated the beginners. I cannot advance their ski-ing unless I get them into the right basic posture and to appreciate why we do certain movements. It means going back to the plough. I hope they don't think it's an insult.'

Nobody did, but this section of our book takes a different form as a consequence. It is more of a report than a graphic analysis, which we will resume in the advanced section.

Our four were average intermediates, probably braver and stronger than most. The first question Ali asked everyone was how they thought a ski turned. These were the responses:

- 'The snow turns the skis.'
- 'My hips move the skis.'
- 'The force exerted by my legs to a degree, in combination with skis and the snow.'
- 'Well, I lean into the hill and just push them round.'

The hazy ideas came out in the way people skied. Elly did move her hips round, which meant she flattened the ski and lost its edging quality. Jim was especially determined to force the skis round. It is the commonest single fault of any intermediate on a plateau.

Ali calls these turns, produced by strong physical effort, 'gorilla turns'. There were a lot of gorilla turns in the first few days, but gradually the basic idea, of the ski as a tool for turning, took hold.

'As soon as they begin to feel the ski working for them,' said Ali, 'half their problems will vanish. They'll develop completely natural body positions as a result of the feedback from their skis, and they'll lose fear.

'Too many systems try to get people through this "panic zone" quickly. They'll realize now that the ski will not be drifting unstably sideways all the time. They'll realize it runs along its length towards the fall line and from the fall line out. The fall line will offer no real fears anymore. It's a secure feeling.

Unlearning

It was hard on the intermediates, having to unlearn. As Corey said, 'The first thing I found out was that I hadn't been ski-ing right for the last 10 years. It's natural we're going through a period of frustration. I'm used to muscling my way down the mountain, looking like a gorilla at times, but I'm going to try hard to learn Ali's finesse.'

False Perceptions

In addition to weight-shift, all the intermediates had the familiar parallel psychosis: they had convinced themselves they were not good skiers unless they held their skis together. They were afflicted much more than the beginners because they had been ski-ing for years, using the conventional vocabulary, and they had seen better skiers whizz down with their skis parallel.

It's only natural to try to ski with legs together after that. But it's a static misinterpretation of a dynamic situation. The faster skier's skis *come* together but are not *brought* together. The moment anyone thinks simply of bringing the skis together, the hip comes across, the turning ski is flattened and control of the turn is lost. There's a big wild skid, which is hard on the muscles and creates insecurity.

Conversely, when the ski is edged properly with

knee, leg and hips held in the right posture, there is more security and it is maintained as the body responds to greater pulling pressures at higher speeds.

Language

As well as the problem of misunderstanding what one sees, there's the problem of mishearing. For years our intermediate skiers had heard injunctions to 'Go up' and 'Go down', for instance. Not surprisingly, there was a tendency to sit down and to stand up.

But what is required in a 'down' movement is a progressive decrease in height brought about only by greater inward leg lean, and not by any significant change in the basic posture. That is, the pelvis, thighs and knees remain forward, unlike the sitting down position.

Ali spent time with the intermediates on reading terrain, allowing them to choose their own line down the mountain, and applying traverse, sideslip and turns as they thought best.

He encouraged them to think out a route and the techniques for it: 'Here's a slope which is not very steep, but it's narrow and there are a couple of bumps. Note that in the middle of the gulley the snow is all scraped away, so there's only ice left. But there's soft snow on the other side of the bumps. Let's sideslip over the ice, and turn by deflection against the back of the bump where the snow is so good.'

For the first part of each day he urged them to choose runs where the snow conditions were likely to be good because of north-facing slopes and to build up technical skills so that by the afternoon they were mentally and physically ready to attempt something tougher.

When they found themselves on icy and crusty slopes they realized that the sounds of scraping were likely to make them tense up defensively. They should resist this defensive reaction. Always, instead of ski-ing straight off, they should do the three exercises of knee push, pole arc, and Ali-lujah.

'Reach out, reach out on the first turn of the morning, it's the turn that can set your ski-ing for the rest of the day.'

EXERCISES FOR INTERMEDIATES

Here are five of the exercises Ali set the intermediates to encourage a feeling for the skis, and to increase confidence and awareness. The first deals with fall-line phobia.

1. Hands on Knees

Ali asked the group to 'short-circuit the brain' by doing a movement without thinking about turning. It was the beginners' exercise of leaning down and gently pressing knee and leg progressively inwards. He put them on a very shallow plough to give stability; it was a minor deviation of the skis.

'All I'm after is to get them in touch with their skis. I don't believe in analyzing every single bit of their ski-ing. There's too much fragmented teaching. It confuses people and keeps them on an ability plateau, whereas once they feel what the ski can do their whole attitude changes.'

Comments on the exercise:

'Jane started bolt upright, not in the 'S' posture. Then she simply made a turn. She didn't hold it in the shallow plough. She twisted her shoulders to face downhill, as she'd been taught. I want her to leave her shoulders alone, and let the hip, the centre of mass, and the leg, do the work. If they're right, the shoulders will be perfect. If the shoulders go wrong, it's because the hips are rotating and they rotate the shoulders.'

'Jim thought he was pushing his knee in, but he used his whole body to drag his skis around. He's a physically strong person and I have to work on him to realize that ski-ing is a delicate, gentle sport and that it's precise, gentle movements that get the best results.'

'Corey had a real fight. He put his ski on its edge nicely but then allowed the momentum to work into the ski. He was still thinking of screwing it round. He's obviously

Below Compare the beginning of the turn, neutral position, and the turning position. The decrease in height is produced only by angulation and not by deliberate down movement.

been taught to 'shift weight' and in his interpretation of that he's flattening the outside ski. It's not wrong to pressurize the outside ski, but his interpretation of it is wrong – and so is the interpretation of most intermediates.'

'Elly also started off by edging the ski nicely and progressively, and the turn started well. Then it suddenly stopped working. The ski went flat again as she thought about shifting her weight on to it. All I was looking for was leg lean. I have somehow to get at the computer punch card which is telling her: 'Plant pole, lift foot, shift weight and rotate round pole.' She'll have to stop using the pole until she can break the habit.'

But Elly sensed what it was all about early on and her elation came through. 'The very first time I pressed my hand on my knee I just felt that the ski was going round the corner, that I was only following it. It felt such an easy, relaxed way of ski-ing compared to what I'd been doing for years, which was heaving myself on a planted pole around the corner. The trouble is that when I get the idea that possibly I might not be getting round that bend, that maybe the inside ski is going to stick, then I go back to my old habits immediately.'

An awareness pointer – imagine you have to sit on an invisible seat at the centre of the turn.

The crouch. You can only make a minimum movement in edge change with such a low position. The exercise is important to 'physical' skiers, like Jim and Corey in the film.

2. Reach Out

The group was asked, when turning, to reach out down the slope with the downhill pole and to draw a long arc in the snow with the spike. It's a variation of the exercise the beginners did to learn the traverse position.

'Reach out!' Ali shouted. Jim found it worked for him: 'I don't know how it looked but it sure felt good. It was a carve. It makes you feel like you are just on the wall of death. You can just feel the ski going right round the mountain.'

3. Reach for the Fall Line

Ali positioned the group on a modest slope but got them into a four o'clock traverse so that they would move at fair speed. Then he asked them simply to stretch upwards and forwards towards the fall line. Hands and poles were to be raised in the air over their heads; they were to commit themselves totally. He didn't tell them what the consequences would be; he wanted them to discover for themselves and not to try any other 'normal' ski movement.

What happened after they moved happily off was that the committed stretching movement changed the edges of the skis: they ran along their length into the fall line. The intermediates made the discovery for themselves that there was no need to heave and shift weight, or to jump, or to do anything violent. The committed, soft, stretching movement was enough to initiate a long curving arc towards the fall line. Once into the fall line, the intermediates controlled their speed and completed the turn by progressively assuming a turning position, knees and hips to the centre of the new turn.

This exercise was a huge success. Ali-lujah! shouted Jane and Elly. The shout matched their elation but, as Ali pointed out later, they should have cried out 'Plum Worrell!' for he was the inventor of the exercise, a Manchester plumber who gave Ali Ross his first lesson on snow. Plum has skied and taught in the Cairngorms for a generation and has a radical approach. Ali developed the exercise from Plum's original idea of raising the arms and doing a swimming breast stroke to turn.

4. Wee Seat

There is nothing more important than getting the hips to the centre of the turn. The exercise to get the right position is to imagine that there is a little seat to the inside of the arc of the turn.

5. The Crouch

The skilful skier, Ali explained, can adjust his body positions and movements to meet the demands of varying terrain. The problem for most middle-of-the-road skiers is their image of a good skier – an upright person with skis glued together. They are frightened to deviate from this, thinking it cannot be right or may look silly.

The crouch exercise demonstrates two things to the skier:

1. Regardless of the body position a change of ski edge will be effective

2. Stabilizing the centre of mass, which is easy at a low position, produces a technically sound turn in which the skier feels secure.

Ali did the crouch, sinking down as low as he possibly could while staying in balance. He let the skis gather speed and then simply changed knee direction while still in the crouch. No up or down movement. He went down the slope making medium radius turns.

It was comic to watch: Ali was almost touching the ground. But the turns were splendid. When the group tried it Jim was the only one who got near the ground and they were the best turns he had done. The others thought they were low down but they weren't. Jane thought she was crouched but she was assuming a reasonable ski-ing position for the first time.

Everyone should try the crouch. At the very least it will shatter the idea that ski-ing is a sport of frozen postures. Exercises like this may seem absurd but they can transform the concept and execution of ski-ing movements.

Summary on the Intermediates

Ali Ross sums up: Our group made progress, more than I expected in the conditions. They had to contend not only with discouraging weather but with the demands of being part of a film. This imposed two extra strains on them – lessons every day and a rather dramatic atmosphere.

My advice to intermediates generally is to have lessons, but not every day. They should spend time on the exercises we did in the filming. They should free-ski on easier runs instead of trying to prove a point by collecting bruises from difficult runs. Nobody learns to ski in a state of fear.

THE INTERMEDIATES COMMENT

I never expected in two weeks to transform the ski-ing of intermediates stuck on a 'plateau', and it was a tribute to them that they achieved as much as they did in trying circumstances. They unlearned, which was the first, hard part; and the good days should multiply as they try out their new thoughts on new snow. Here is what they would like to pass on to other intermediates:

JANE:

My basic problem, probably quite a common one, was that as soon as conditions became difficult I would lean in to the hill and lose control.

The exercise that helped most was to stretch to full height with the arms downhill: it literally threw me into a position totally dedicated to a turn. It's also very relaxing, builds up a good rhythm and allows speed to increase without fear. I always kept this exercise in my head if I was stiff or the going was tough. I might do it without raising my arms, simply by thinking of standing on my toes and falling into the turn.

I feel that my ski-ing became far more flowing and quite effortless, even on pistes which would normally have caused a problem. I appreciated for the first time how little effort is required to make the ski work for you.

ELLY

I knew it would be very difficult for me to let go of the safety holds which were the only way I knew to ski: when you're on a steep mountain feeling safe is all that matters in life. It took a tremendous effort to force myself to let go of the old way which had kept me safe but also stiff and horribly stylized, like a doll.

If I actually thought of moving on to the upper edge in order to turn I couldn't do it, but if I made an arc with a ski pole I felt I was gliding. The other image that helped me was to float in the turn with my arms raised above my head – what we called the Ali-lujah position!

I like the idea of making an overall movement instead of subdividing fragments of technique. I've done three years of intensive contemporary dance which is all working in images and the best dance teachers cultivate this same unbitty approach. It was the most beautiful feeling of all in the learning process, not least because by then I knew how lovely it was to be going round the arc when I 'came back' and edged the skis.

The catchwords which did the most for me were 'commit' and 'edge'. I said them aloud and said them a bit softer when people were around. I knew it

worked for the slow narrow plough turn but I needed to command myself. In my old ways the accent had been on the lower ski and I'd automatically lifted the upper ski. Thinking back, I can see it never occurred to me to think about weighting.

That flying image gave me more confidence than anything else. I clung to it after the first time because I hadn't been scared at that point of the turn. I felt safe again, knowing I could come out of the downhill flying pose whenever I wanted. That the flying was to allow us to change the edge of the ski was a secondary matter: ski-ing became a flowing dance.

I mustn't forget the other things I learned, such as being aware of the terrain and other people — like poking the lift man with my ski pole again and again because I was so excited about the ski-ing!

JIM:
I understand the vital necessity of being relaxed, not only in ski-ing but in most sports, but I was programmed from the start to give the course everything I had. It goes without saying that the awareness that our ski-ing was about to be aired to

The exercises on pp. 81-83 are what helps intermediates to get off the ability plateau.

thousands of viewers in itself caused an amount of unnecessary anxiety.

The little drills we went through were a tremendous help. Each time you see it done properly the technique is planted deeper in your mind and sooner or later you'll get it spot on, but most of the times when Ali noticed me ski-ing better, I felt no different. Maybe Olivia Newton John should take film of me ski-ing and use that with her song 'Let's Get Physical'.

COREY:
My main problem was relying on strength rather than on the ski and on finesse. Ali's opening advice on the contour of the ski and using it to turn created an indelible impression. This information, coupled with the exercise to push the outside leg inward to make a turn, was really beneficial in getting the feel of the ski turning.

I also liked the exercise where we held our poles outwards and then reached down to strike the correct body position. Ali's emphasis on beginning the turn early was vital (though sometimes easily forgotten!).

With moguls, I was helped by Ali's instruction to survey the slope first and then to plant the pole on the peak of the mogul, allowing the skis to take you round.

IN POWDER IN THE ROCKIES

We were joined in the mountains in Vail by Horst Abraham, the guru of American ski teaching. He skied the powder with Ali Ross and the group.
'The real magic of ski-ing,' says Horst, 'transcends the zigging and zagging of the skis. It's the feeling: I'm flying, I'm in control of my own destiny. This wonderful, difficult-to-describe feeling of "My gosh, this is me".'

ADVANCED SKI-ING IN VAIL

We went West to Colorado for the final two programmes in the TV series on advanced ski-ing. The lure was the powder snow of the Rockies. In the high dry air it falls light, silky and soft—you can swing a ski pole through it and feel no resistance. We were soon up to our knees in the lovely stuff in Vail and Beaver Creek. Vail offers beautifully groomed slopes but there were steep mogul fields as well to test the best of us. Five advanced skiers were selected in Vail, three Americans and two English. From the left:

Di:

I'm 28, and work for Ski Promotions in London. I began with the book *We Learned to Ski* nearly ten years ago. I want to gain stability and safety at speed, reduce my fear of ice and learn control through the bumps.

Bridget:

I'm 50 and a hostess at the Lodge in Vail. I was born in England and ice-skated professionally for 11 years. I sort of tussle down the slope like a little old lady and I'd love just to come zipping down and really go for the mountain.

Bill:

I'm 34, a plumber. I've skied for 22 years, but I've stuck to just ski-ing the groomed slopes and I want to be able to ski powder well. I'm an introvert, but ski-ing brings out my other, exhibitionist side.

Ellen:

I'm 26, a marketing consultant and writer. I've skied 8 years and want to overcome the fear I feel when ski-ing in deep powder and on steep slopes. I've been told I have multiple sclerosis, but I refuse to accept that.

Gary:

I'm 33, a master carpenter. All my ski-ing ability comes from just watching other good skiers; I've never had a formal lesson. I like being able to go out and experience the outback in the winter and have a mode of transportation. The ultimate dance...ski-ing is the ultimate dance with the mountain.

BACK TO BASICS

Most skiers looking at the five who joined our advanced group in Vail would admire them for their stylish performance. They were all competent skiers, capable of getting down any piste. But they themselves knew their limitations, though not the nature of them. When the going got rough, in heavy snow or off-piste or in steep mogul fields, they knew they tended to go to pieces mentally and technically. Hence their enthusiasm for taking their ski-ing apart.

Their misunderstandings were the same, though the expression of them varied according to their characters.

Bill had an obsession with looking good and this got in the way of what creates good-looking ski-ing. Is it not enough to feel good?

Di, though technically the best skier, seemed to be interpreting a series of static images.

Bridget was taught for many years that a good skier had to be aggressive, which is misleading because the idea of aggression tends to produce exaggerated movements. I asked her to think of 'commitment' rather than 'aggression'.

Ellen was skilful in her performance but had a deep fear based on lack of

knowledge: she had never really experienced what the ski could do.

Gary, who had never had a lesson in his life, was a strong skier, enthusiasm and commitment to the

mountains overcoming practical shortcomings in technique.

I put the advanced skiers on to the narrow plough for the same reason as I did the intermediates. Their conception of parallel ski-ing was the trouble. Their objective was to have the legs together; as a result they felt insecure on anything other than a perfect piste.

My first aim was to get them to understand and feel how the ski turns towards the fall line. Their habit was to jump or rotate the ski, for which the ski had to be flat. I wanted them to realize that by a committed edge-change movement, the ski would

take them to the fall line.

The parallel is not a special turn in this respect. In every turn so far described the ski has been made to travel along its own length. I see no necessity to change this.

Indeed, the advanced skier attempting to go faster, and in powder snow, cannot cope unless the ski does travel its length.

The reason for starting with the narrow plough (or basic swing turn) is that less commitment is necessary to feel what happens in the final form. None of the advanced skiers felt the anxiety they might have, had I simply said they must commit themselves to the fall line

with their skis together. And had they started with their skis together, you can bet your Western boots they would have performed their normal rotation for a turn.

Nothing is lost by trying the turn with a small opening of the skis. Such is the myth of the

parallel, however, that any deviation of the skis is regarded as incompetent. But, as I explained to Bill, it was not regression at all to do this exercise. The turn with skis deviated at the beginning was the same in essential respects as the true parallel he so admired. (In fact, the most efficient way to ski is by deviating the skis from each other; witness the racers with their step turns.)

The comparisons on this page between the plough (top picture) and the parallel prove the point. The only difference is that in the basic swing the edge change is procured by the deviation, and in the

Note the leg-lean in the basic swing (above) and in the parallel — the same.

parallel it comes about by a very committed leg-leaning movement to the centre of the new turn.

Our advanced group began to get the feel after a couple of runs on good terrain. I didn't tell them to stop deviating the skis: they thought they were still beginning the turn that way. But because of feedback from the edged turning ski they became more secure and began to make more committed movements. As a result they shed the narrow plough without really being aware of it. Once they felt secure the fall line was no longer a panic zone, it was part of the arc of the turn. So gradually they lost their rotating habits.

When we moved to steeper slopes, they had to learn to control their speed. This was achieved by getting them to tighten the radius of the end of the turn. Imagine the sharp curve at the end of a fish-hook; that was the pattern we sought. It was achieved by quicker progressive inward leg-lean, producing more and more edging. Where they might previously have skidded sideways a lot, or jumped the skis round, they were riding round on their edges.

We had next to carry these principles into fall-line and deep-snow ski-ing.

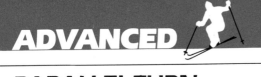
PARALLEL TURN

The critical position at the beginning of the turn with hips and legs to the centre of the turn.

There is nothing new on these pages! I say that in order to try, yet again, to demythologize the parallel turn. It's only a small modification of the plough technique and posture, but because I am travelling at speed in this sound position the skis come together. The togetherness of the skis is not the most important factor in these photographs; it's a consequence of the positions and the movements. Note, above all, the angulation.

93

THE NATURAL PARALLEL

I have skied with mountain guides and crack Alpine skiers in really difficult terrain, and I know they never think about keeping their skis together. When you look at the top racers – the best skiers in the world – you see that they make stepping turns with their skis apart: ski-ing with their legs together is of no importance to them.

I guaranteed all the advanced group in Vail that they would be better parallel skiers if they forgot about it and concentrated on gaining the feeling of the ski simply gliding through and into the fall line: 'After three or four turns, if it's going well, your skis will float together.'

All of them had difficulty at first, because they felt that as advanced skiers they must be parallel skiers the whole time.

Di skied the longer turns well but in fall-line ski-ing the outside ski started to break away. This was because she was not *progressively* increasing her inward leg lean.

Bill was the same. In his case the idea of shifting weight caused the hips to move and the outside ski to flatten: I could see him struggling with a flat skid.

Gary flattened the ski the moment he deliberately moved one ski to join the other. Gary, in fact, raised a common problem: 'It feels good for me to turn one way but my other turn feels really awkward.'

Most skiers have a strong and a weak side: Bridget rotated her body on the weak side in an effect to make the skis come round.

I tried to correct this weakness by emphasising our awareness exercises and by splitting the turn into a beginning and a completion. I got the

To really master the
mountain a skier has to be
able to ski the fall line. This
means coming straight
down in rhythmic turns
with no traversing. There
are numerous areas —
narrow gullies and bump
runs — where fall-line
ski-ing is the most efficient
way down — and, in some
cases, the only way down,
short of sideslipping.

The difference between
the long-radius turn and
the fall-line turn is in the
trajectory of the body. In
the long turn the body
follows the line of the skis,
whereas in the fall-line
turn the body stays facing
down the fall line
throughout. As we tighten
our turns, to control speed,
the trajectory of the body
begins to be more and
more a straight line down
the fall line, with the skis
turning either side of this
line.

To get our advanced
skiers to learn fall-line
turns I first got them to
make loopy turns —
somewhere in between
the line of turning in the
illustration (on this page). I
wanted to develop
confidence for the
commitment you see in a
good skier, whose fall-line
ski-ing appears to be light
and easy.

Begin in a stable
hip-width stance. If we
start off with feet close
together, the inside leg
restricts the working of the
outside, turning leg.

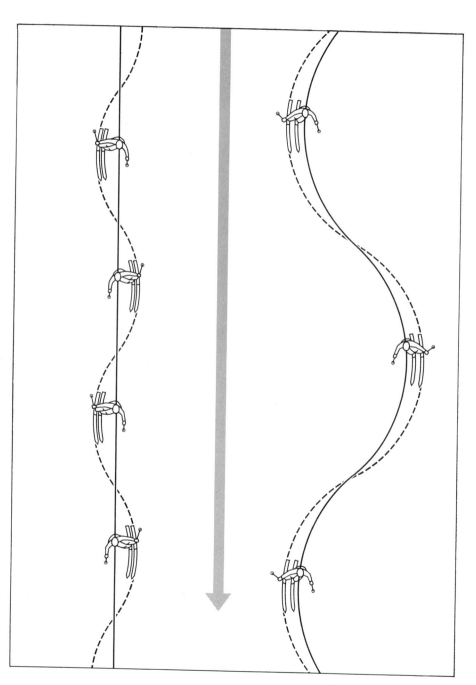

BASIC SHORT TURN

It has to be admitted that fall-line ski-ing takes coordination and a great deal of practice on easy slopes where there is no anxiety about commitment. Everyone in our advanced group had difficulties in stabilizing the upper body. It tended to follow the path of the skis, so that the coiled spring effect was lost and the next turn had to be started by physical input. Then it became tough going.

At this stage in advanced ski-ing we must seriously consider a training programme. We won't get better unless we train physically and mentally, especially when we ski only two weeks in the year. It's extraordinary what people expect their bodies to do without that preparation. Give yourself a chance by warming up when you get off the ski-lift in the morning. Think of the positions and movements you are about to make and give muscles and ligaments a bit of notice. Learn to adapt what works on an easier slope to work on bumps or in steep narrow gullies.

All the elements are now in place – theoretically at least! – to carry us on to bump and

98

result – a series of basic short turns coming down the fall line. Points to note:

1. There are two positions, the turning position and the neutral.

2. In the turning position we are building up the coiled spring; in the neutral position the spring is released and the edges change.

3. After the edges are changed the knees go inwards and forwards to complete the turn the other side

Normally I have advocated controlling speed simply by tightening the turn with progressive inward leg-lean and the skis on edge. But to keep control on steeper and more difficult slopes and in hard or icy snow, we have to modify our turns and allow a certain amount of skid at the end of them. If we skid too much, though, we lose our coiled spring effect and the following turn will have to be started by physical input. This then makes fall-line ski-ing difficult and tiring. The greatest controlling factor should still be the radius of our turn and when we do skid we should set our edges quite positively at the end to produce a rebound which aids control and helps to start our next turn.

FALL-LINE SKI-ING: THE COILED SPRING

I am like a coiled spring in the fall-line turn below. My skis are crossing the trajectory of my upper body. I am resisting the turning effect of the skis because I am keeping my upper body pointing down the fall line (note how I am sitting on the wee seat). I am using my arms as stabilizers. Energy is therefore built up in my torso. It will be released positively to initiate my new turn.

Stefan Zurcher, in the picture on the right, demonstrates the next phase. His body, like mine, is pointing down the fall line with his skis going across. But he has just planted his pole and put pressure on it. This is the trigger which releases the coiled spring of the torso.

The legs swivel towards the fall line. This simple reaction facilitates edge change followed by a strong precise knee movement forward and inward to carry through the turning process on the other side. There is very little physical input. We are using the forces that already exist. All I am required to do — apart from getting my timing right! — is to keep the upper body stabilized. I don't provide any direct physical turning input. That comes from the coiled spring.

Try to visualize the skis curving and running forwards either side of the trajectory of the body, and not being swung or pushed from side to side, which is the popular misconception of good fall-line ski-ing.

The skis crossing the trajectory of the upper body creates the torsional effect.

The body follows the fall line, the skis shoot forward for a moment before the edges change.

BUMP OR MOGUL SKI-ING

While we were in Vail we filmed mogul racers. These are not, of course, oil company chairmen in a hurry, but young people who ski bumps for fun and for prizes. In the course of it they do deliberately what many people do accidentally, which is to take to the air. It's easy to get out of control.

Bumps merely provide more dramatic demonstration of the fact that most bad ski-ing habits develop in response to awkward terrain when we are not ready for it. As soon as we are told 'Now you have to turn' – and mogul fields are full of such messages – we invariably produce the wrong reaction. So the first lesson of mogul ski-ing is to develop perception, to look and think ahead.

There are several ways to get through a mogul field, which will be described on the following pages.

As so often in ski-ing, what we see is misleading. The mogul basher may come straight down, and eventually you may choose to do that too, but it's not the way to begin to come to terms with moguls. For a start, recognize that some mogul fields are not for ski-ing. Those on steeper slopes which have been skied a lot become mountainous and almost impossible; I'd rather go round them and

take another route, unless there is a flowing, smooth line through them. Nothing is proved by terrifying oneself just to be able to say, 'I did it.' On the contrary, you can undo a lot of good basic work on technique – two or three days may be needed to replenish skill and nerve. Learning always takes place in a friendly environment.

Start, therefore, in a sheltered area where the moguls are minor. The easiest way is to traverse across, losing height with sideslip. It's not necessary at this stage to attempt the dynamic postures required for absorbing bumps at speed.

But take a look at the snow conditions. You will find that the downhill side of most bumps, because of the way they have been formed by skiers making turns, are steep and scraped bare of all soft snow. But on the uphill side of the bump towards you, you'll see all that nice snow deposited in a banked heap just waiting for someone to turn in it. We'll go into that in a moment, but start also by having confidence in your skis. As I insist all the way through this book, skis are designed with moguls and other hazards in mind. They will not stick into the side of a bump and stop dead there – they will flex and carry you through.

COMMITMENT IN THE BUMPS

Terms first. The trough is the groove between bumps. As you look down the slope you are looking at the back of all the bumps; the 'front' of each bump faces down the slope.

So, it's time to turn. The aim is to make our way down through the troughs, deflecting off the soft snow at the back of the bumps. We do not necessarily follow the fall line at this stage; it's good to take a breather by traversing and sideslipping to find a line for the next series of turns through the troughs.

The turn is initiated from the back of a bump by projecting knees and hips toward the fall line; once the turn has begun we complete in the normal way. We may be afraid in the fall line but it's fatal to turn too quickly through it at this stage. If we do, we will end up on the very steep, icy and scraped front side of the bump which started our turn on.

The pole is not an embellishment in mogul ski-ing: it is vital. It provides an aid to timing and also a support at the stage of commitment. In the photograph I am at the start of a turn in bumps. My body is facing my new direction of travel, in anticipation of where the skis are going to be and I plant the pole firmly on the back of the bump.

There is impact caused by momentum as pole touches snow. We must prepare to meet this impact by stiffening the arm. Unless we do so the tendency is for the impact to rotate the shoulders, lessening the coiled spring effect.

Commitment is required in the bumps at the stage of projecting the knees and hips forward toward the fall line. But this must not be confused with 'aggression', which is so often mentioned with bump ski-ing of all kinds. I believe aggression is unhelpful. It conjures up an atmosphere of hostility and with it of fear. There certainly is fear in ski-ing the bumps: all our advanced skiers experienced it and I had no difficulty in understanding it. But I don't think you can banish fear by attacking something.

I don't feel aggressive when I ski the bumps well. I don't find the idea of hacking the mountain to pieces particularly attractive. I find it more helpful to think of caressing my way through a field of bumps. I know a lot of good skiers who say they 'fight' their way down a mountain, but I think it's a shame to connect such a beautiful sport with aggression, and it certainly can produce the wrong effects.

The black line shows the route for the less competent skier traversing and side slipping and looking for a friendly bump to turn on. The grey line shows the route for the more confident and skilful skier closer to the fall line.

FALL-LINE SKI-ING IN THE BUMPS

Two basic mistakes had to be eliminated in the early bump ski-ing – an eagerness to turn too quickly and get it over with; and a tendency to turn along the crest, with the result that people ended up going faster and faster and out of control.

The next stage of development was to learn how to cope with speed. It was at this point that I introduced the ideas of absorbing and stretching.

Absorbing
This means allowing the legs to fold up in response to impact, soaking it up.

Stretching
This follows absorption; it means extending the legs to maintain ski-snow contact (and without that you cannot turn effectively).

We began practising absorption and stretching without turning, beginning on the last half-dozen bumps when I knew there was a piece of flat terrain coming where we could let the skis run out and stop easily. On the second attempt I might try eight bumps, on the third twelve, and so on, until we were nearly running the whole bump-slope straight, absorbing and stretching as we came down. The knowledge that they could accomplish this equipped my group completely for the next step, which was to add

This is a technically good absorption- stretch sequence. But again it's an example of the difficulty of understanding what we see. I appear to be deliberately sitting back. I'm not. It's the impact of the bump which tends to push me back. I remain in dynamic balance.

turning movements to absorption and stretching.

We brought to bump ski-ing in the fall line the techniques used in straight fall-line ski-ing. But it must be emphasized that it is possible to analyze and intellectualize too much. It's an odd observation, perhaps, for a book on learning to ski, but by this stage in ski-ing you must be reacting to what you see and feel. It is not possible to ski the bumps, and enjoy them, if you are trying to cope with a set of fragmented injunctions.

I advocate perception training. Choose a section of the slope, preferably with a run-out. Work out the line for fall-line ski-ing with turns. Think about what you want to do. Then do it.

We talked in Vail to one of the champion mogul racers. 'Before I take off I'm concentrating on checking out my line. My knees do most of the absorbing as I come over a bump. I find that the more you can absorb at the back and extend into the troughs the faster you can go, the more ski-snow contact you get. The biggest factor in mogul ski-ing is to stay forward on your skis because once you start sitting back you start sliding. I practise by keeping my feet apart, doing it more slowly, and getting an independent edge feel.'

A classic series of bump turns demonstrating all the ingredients of good fall-line ski-ing plus the absorption and extension techniques necessary for good ski-snow contact. Compress on the bumps, extend in the troughs.

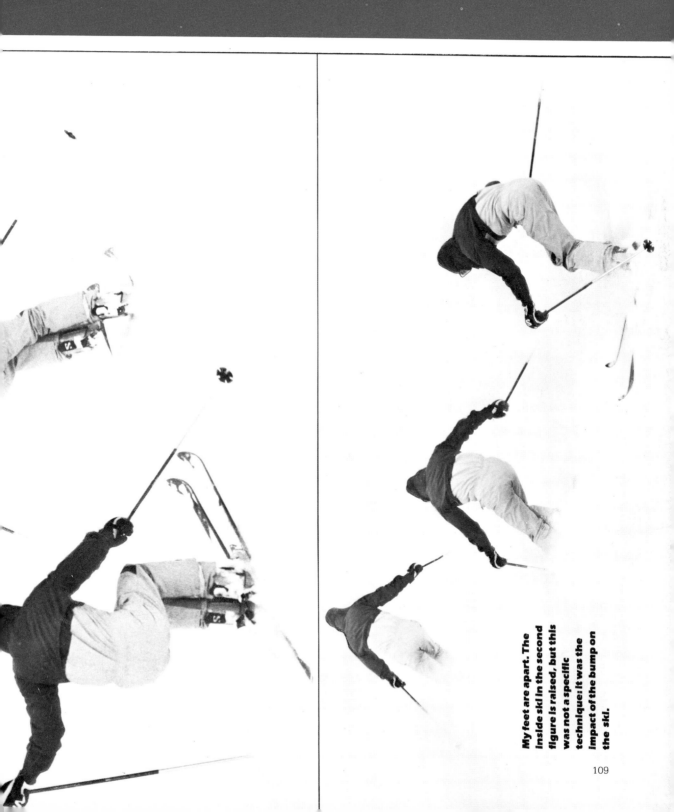

My feet are apart. The inside ski in the second figure is raised, but this was not a specific technique: it was the impact of the bump on the ski.

THE CLASS IN BUMPS AND POWDER

There were snowfalls of about a metre (2 to 3ft) during the advanced course in Vail, and everybody was rather tense when we went to the top at Beaver Creek and looked down the wide trails with moguls undulating in the powder.

Fear in powder and in the bumps was the main obstacle for the advanced skiers, as they tried to rush through the fall line. But, one morning, they realized they needed the speed of the fall line in order to turn in deep powder. As soon as they had the confidence to let the skis ride into the fall line, I could see them beginning to enjoy the sensation of the skis turning in an arc with the inward leg lean.

Fear returned when we went off-piste, but the slope was no steeper than any the group had done.

Ellen said: 'I know it's only psychological. Because it's an ungroomed slope I think I shouldn't be able to ski it and that psyched me out.

I never thought I would lose my fear of powder, but I have.

It's finding that bit of extra nerve to let the skis gather speed for two or three seconds in the fall line before you complete the turn. I've never done it like this before in my whole life.'

Di said: 'Before I was putting in 70% of my effort at the beginning of the turn and very little at the end. Now I realize I can use the mogul to help turn the ski and change its edge, and I put in the effort at the end of the turn to control myself. I'm learning to get control of the moguls that way.'

Bridget said: 'I just gritted my teeth and thought I'll show the whole damn lot! It was such an effort before and now I don't feel the strain any

more.'

Bill, who would be admired by most tourist skiers for his style and dash, admitted he found it hard to maintain the light and gentle approach to turning: 'When I'm tense I find that I go back to being physical again, like I've been for 22 years. I think it has something to do with the camera sitting and waiting to catch me in a ski-ing position!'

Bill also had a little difficulty with excising all trace of the idea of 'unweighting'. Most skiers of his experience were brought up with the theory that they had to unweight the skis and then transfer the weight for the turn. I want them to rise up and feel light in the fall line. Anything else leads to excess physical movements.

I understood Bill's point of view but it was very important to keep insisting that he shed his thought of weighting and unweighting.

Bill found it helpful to concentrate on just one arc of a turn. At the end of the powder run he commented: 'The old brain took over there. I couldn't have lasted another 50 metres because I was putting too much effort into it.'

Gary also noticed the difference between letting the skis work and following old habits: 'I'm finding it a lot easier to ski the bumps in this deep new snow. Everything is cushioned; it slows the whole thing down. It's like doing everything in slow motion compared to hard-packed snow. My first turns were a bit physical. By that I mean I just physically cranked myself round, but in the open I decided to let my skis run and it became smooth and effortless.'

DEEP SNOW

What *is* it we're afraid of, I asked. Fear of falling? Or, as Bill perceptively put it, fear of being seen to fall? Fear of injury? I didn't regard these fears as unhealthy. There's a reality to some fear which calls for a prudent response: blind courage, which takes a good skier on to a slope set for an avalanche, or makes a poor skier a liability to himself

reasonable speed without coming out.

This is also a demonstration of the fact that I have not been exerting rotational force to the skis. It is a good test for anyone because it analyzes how you are ski-ing. If you're ski-ing well, most of the movements should be lateral and therefore the binding should hold you,

rescue in the end because a six-mile walk in deep powder is too much for almost anyone. Straps are necessary, fairly long ones to eliminate the possibility of being hit by a loose ski. Some resorts also sell a red marker cord which unwinds when the ski comes off.

This leaves the risk of falling – and once your bindings are set right that

We all took spills to remove the fear of falling. Remove the fear of *failing* by leaving your aesthetic image on the piste.

and other skiers, is not much use.

The real risks require a positive response. First, the risk of injury. When I ski powder and bumps I set my bindings back at least one notch. I often do an experiment. I set the bindings back to zero: the modern bindings have such elasticity and qualities of shock absorption that I can ski down a difficult run at a

even at zero.

I don't advocate ski-ing powder and bumps at zero, however: one notch down is about right for most people. That cuts the risk of injury and should give confidence.

A second real risk is losing a ski in deep snow. I've seen thoughtless people stuck for hours looking for a lost ski, having to call out mountain

is the source of the most unnecessary fear. I spent half a day making everyone tumble in the snow, playing in it, taking flips and having snowball fights. At first they were tense as they fell. Then they realized that powder snow is soft. They fell and they fell just for the fun of it. A major inhibition to powder ski-ing vanished in their yells and laughter.

THE SKIS STILL WORK...

There is some practical value in those pretty postcards of the tracks left by good skiers in powder: they are a series of curves. The clue to the way the ski works in powder is there for everyone to see. There is little evidence of any sideslipping: the depth of the snow alone will not permit the ski to go sideways.

Think of the ski running along its length through the snow and meeting very little resistance. Let that image obliterate the false one of the skier pushing his feet from side to side. This is a view from in front; if you were poised above a good powder skier you would see him riding an arc.

There are four other delusions.

The first is that the skis will not turn in powder. This increases fear of the fall line – people want to get out of it as quickly as possible, hence they jump around and rotate the hips. The skis cross and we have our first typical deep snow fall.

The second delusion arises from the misconception of how the ski turns. On-piste it is possible to get the skis round simply by shifting weight to the turning ski, producing a sideways skid. In deep snow, skidding is not possible: the shift of weight to the outside ski just makes it sink in the snow. The skier performs the classic deep snow fall to the outside.

The third delusion is related to the second and lies in the popular expression that in powder one shifts one's weight to both skis.

Forget about weight-shifting and forget about unweighting. An interpretation of what is required to take weight off skis or to shift weight can lead us to do things which are no help. It happens that in soft snow there is no real base and it is this which decides that the weight distribution is equal on both feet.

The pressure of the pull to the outside of a turn distributes itself fairly evenly on both skis – but you don't put it there. It is a terribly unnecessary thing to think about, and we come back to the same old story: if we make the right decisions and the right movements, and allow the skis to do the work for us, we will make effective turns regardless of conditions and snow depth.

The fourth delusion is that good skiers sit back. It may be necessary at the beginning of a run to adjust one's weight ever so slightly backwards to raise the tips out of the snow and gather speed, but once we have ski-ing speed we must feel we are in balance. So how is it that the powder hounds seem to be sitting back and some of them even believe they are sitting back?

There are two explanations. The first, and the most important, is analyzed in our drawing of the end of a turn. The skis sink in the snow and tips come forward; as this happens the skis are in a shallower angle in relationship to the slope than they would be if the skier was on hard snow.

The second reason is that the skier has to anticipate the effect of inertia at the finish of a turn. Anyone who tries to sit back and ski powder will soon feel the effect on burning muscles: he'll be worn out after a couple of runs. Soft snow requires us to remain in dynamic balance.

I've no idea who first made the observations, but when I work I often think of these sentences: I hear and forget; I see and remember; I do and I understand. My other idea is that one picture is worth a thousand words, but I will add to that – as long as we understand the picture!

So, practise positions in front of a mirror; when you're at a resort, see if you can get yourself filmed to play back on video. Watch the good skiers and try to feel what you see.

I give some exercises on the next page to help, but I do want to encourage you not to get bogged down by too much fragmentation, in what is surely a sport whose name is freedom.

The angle of the skis to the slope surface creates an illusion of sitting back.

As long as we understand the picture...As in all good fall-line ski-ing, the momentum of our body running down the fall line assists the initiation of the next turn.

ENJOYING THE POWDER

The advanced skiers looked at me with incredulity when I told them we would use exactly the same techniques as the beginners and intermediates. A great deal of bull is talked about powder, almost as if powder skiers wanted to put other people off and boost their own egos.

I began the powder training by asking everyone to form a small V with their skis. I wanted them to realize for themselves that regardless of the deep snow the ski would still work. We went through all the exercises described in the earlier part of this book.

It is extremely demanding to try ski-ing slowly through deep snow and as they built up confidence, I got them to go faster. Until we come to terms with the idea that speed replaces physical input, we will never cope with soft-snow ski-ing.

But even the advanced skiers had to be coaxed into that, and the best way of doing it, I have found, is to use the Reach for the Fall Line exercise I have described earlier – the Plum Worrell turn or the Ali-lujah position as Elly and Jane called it.

In powder you must begin on a steep traverse and be going at reasonable speed. The crucial thing is the direction in which you rise. Merely to stretch upwards will have no effect unless you stretch towards the fall line and stretch with the legs as well as the body.

Think of a line between your toe binding and the tip of the ski pointing downhill to the centre of the next turn. It is this forward stretch which changes the edges of the skis and allows them to curve along their edges to the fall line.

The moment the turn begins you make it flow. Remember the clockface. You never stop moving throughout the radius of the turn. There is a progressive change in posture with greater inward leg-lean.

But, please, let's not overcomplicate the joy of going through powder snow. To stand on your skis and let them run straight through powder on a friendly slope is one of the most beautiful feelings I know.

Ellen summed up some good days in the powder: 'It's so light and fluffy; why was I afraid of it in the first place?'

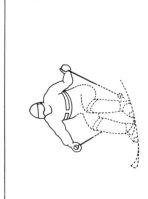

Preparation and pole plant. The apparent sitting back is due to the resistance of the snow.

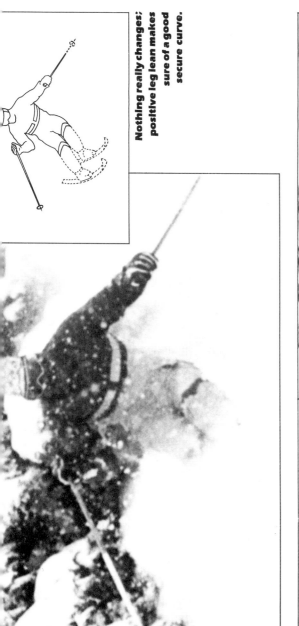

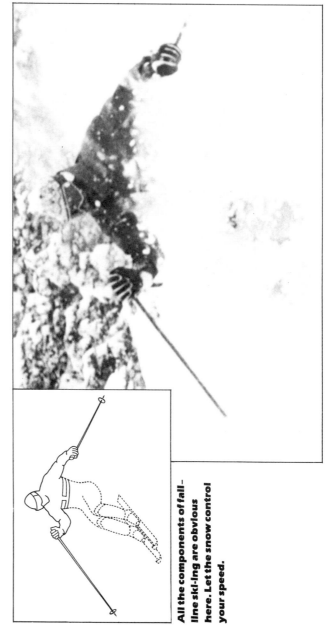

Nothing really changes: positive leg lean makes sure of a good secure curve.

All the components of fall-line ski-ing are obvious here. Let the snow control your speed.

CONCLUSIONS FROM THE ADVANCED CLASS

I couldn't alter a lifetime's ski-ing habits of the group in two weeks but everyone made an important piece of progress – becoming aware of their body positions.

I think first of Ellen. I didn't know at the beginning about her incipient sclerosis. She skied much more smoothly at the end.

Bridget's age became less of a handicap to her. Fear started to disappear when she found something was going to work, and even on her less efficient right turn I could see a definite naturalness appearing most of the time in good conditions.

Gary surprised me most because he is a big, strong man, but he did learn to limit physical effort.

Most people would be thrilled if they could ski half as well as Di, but her real progress will come next year as she skis more and thinks more about what we've been doing.

As for Bill – one of these days he'll stop giving himself a hard time, like so many skiers who worry about appearance, and then he'll surprise himself. We asked the advanced group to comment on their experience for the benefit of other skiers. The shortest summary came from Bill, who simply said: 'Limit physical input.' But if that is a cryptic comment it is a valid one, since most intermediate and advance skiers still have too much upper body movement.

Di thought the little trick which helped her most was thinking of a 'wee seat' to the centre of the turn which made her keep her hips and centre of mass in the right position. Also: 'I was previously unaware that my arms blocked my next turn and that I was therefore producing too much effort.

Now, by using a more open upper body stance, as if ready to pounce down the fall line, I find that initiating the turn has become less of an effort and more a matter of changed edges – floating into the fall line, and then increasing edge pressure by knee and ankle angulation to complete and control the turn.'

Gary's view was 'What I have learnt most is posture – what to do with my frame, my skeleton. I try now to keep my body pointing downhill when I am ski-ing the fall line. I remember to keep my knees in front. That's really helped me in my ski-ing because I feel more balanced.'

Bridget: 'I've learnt to run the knees into the fall line to get the ski in the right position, and then let them do the work for me. It really does feel good when that happens. I'd like to ski until I am over 70, because at 70 you get free lift tickets!'

Ellen triumphed over her 'nagging little problem', as she refers to the multiple sclerosis. 'They say we should have a life without stress and rest a lot, but that's totally against my nature. I make a conscious effort to keep my muscles working and to stretch. I do aerobics. I went through a period when I would fall downstairs and run into walls and had no coordination whatsoever. Now I am much more conscious of every move I make and of where my body is. I can't deny that things do happen sometimes when I get a weakness in my leg and a numbness in my hand. But I shall never end up in a wheelchair if willpower has anything to do with it. I will keep on ski-ing.'

LEARNING TO SKI:

A CONVERSATION BETWEEN ALI ROSS AND HORST ABRAHAM

Horst Abraham is the leading light of American ski teaching, president of the American Federation of Ski Teachers and the author of an acclaimed book, *Skiing Right*. One evening, after they had been ski-ing together in the powder, Horst and Ali talked about the way people learn to ski and about their own attitudes to teaching.

Ali: I was 18 when I really started ski-ing. The systems for teaching in those days were very pedantic but we learned somehow, and I remember vividly going back and trying to copy the shapes and positions I had seen good skiers adopt. I stood in front of a mirror to do it, but today there's video to help.

Horst: I started to ski at 2½! Later I was inducted first into the Austrian system, then the German system, then the French system and then the American system. But I still didn't know how to teach, and I most certainly didn't know how to ski. That all happened only after I'd sat back and reflected on the experiences and discovered what I call intuitive effectiveness—turning my awareness to the inside. I believe we learn through a variety of senses. Video feed-back from tape or film may be meaningful to some. To others it's the muscles which tell them where they are—the pressure on the foot and so on. And there are some people who are more auditory and listen to what the skis sound like on the snow. Teaching should really address itself to conveying messages to all these senses.

Ali: I think we can take it a stage further. A lot of ski schools don't even ask the question 'How do people learn?' It's rather that they say, 'This is how we teach.' That's the end of it—if it's not written in their book of teaching, it can't be acceptable. Well, I don't think a professional teacher should tell a beginner he can teach him to ski as he does. I'd prefer him to say he can teach people to enjoy it the same way.

Take an example. If we look at normal instruction we find that a very standard phrase is to tell the learner to put pressure on his outside ski. The average person's understanding of putting pressure on the outside ski comes from walking around every day in life, shifting pressure from one foot to another. If somebody says you must shift your weight to your outside ski, they will do it in the only way they know how, and usually that's to move across on to that ski. Which flattens it, and a flat ski is a load of trouble to an average person ski-ing down a mountain. It just goes sideways. To make the problem worse, the information is received in a static mode but must be put into practice in a dynamic mode—while ski-ing. If people don't grasp the difference between static and dynamic, then their understanding is going to be delayed.

Horst: Looking at some of the very fine skiers on the Vail slopes today, I couldn't help but notice their skill and coordination. Where do these come from? From within — an idea, a concept of flow. Coordination is certainly not the linking of fragmented sequences, it's an intuitive expression of something. If teachers adopt a series of sequences, or segments, and try to make that the basis of coordination, they're fooling themselves. They don't know about learning. The good teacher needs to make other people feel good about themselves. I want to bring the student to an unconscious level of competence. For instance, teach me how to get out of this chair. Go ahead! It would take us all night! We're just stuffing our students full of dos and don'ts, shoulds and ifs. No wonder we constipate them to the point of paralysis!

Ali: I agree. You've seen total beginners learning to walk on skis. They've been told to take their right pole and plant it opposite their left foot. One of our beginners, Keith, tried to do this on the first day and just couldn't work it out. The following day he just put his skis on and off he went, walking with a totally normal arm-stick movement. One of the demands of a ski teacher's examination is to walk 'correctly' on skis. The rules demand that you plant the right pole, point it towards the rear of your ski, and at the same time as you pull on it your left leg moves forward. Incredible. Even people at ski teacher level get it wrong. It's this stress on fragmented learning which is one of our problems in teaching people to ski.

Horst: Right. I really feel in a way that the ultimate performance comes from intellectual ignorance, that when you're ski-ing you don't in fact 'think' about your movements; you feel them. If, say, you begin to wonder, 'What if over that edge there's a grizzly bear waiting for me' — you won't be able to move very easily!

Ali: I agree that thought process can control how well people behave — I was afraid a couple of times today because I didn't know what was over the edge; it's a very inhibiting factor for someone learning. They might ski very well on the prepared surface and then go to pieces on another slope which is no steeper but just happens to be off the piste.

Horst: After all, what is ski-ing? It's all the things that your job and daily life don't allow you to do. It's cutting loose; it's being yourself and honest. Most people start a bit apprehensive: they don't want to batter themselves to death. On their vacation they'd like to experience success, the kind of success they may be deprived of in a job. They want to say 'I can' rather than 'I can't.' This is really the therapeutic value of ski-ing: you rediscover yourself. I believe the majority of people have a defensive attitude and in ski-ing they can overcome this and learn to think of themselves as winners.

Ali: I rarely free-ski with other people but when I do, with people like Stefan Zurcher, Rene Seiler and you, I'm brought to a new level of awareness. When I follow you down the mountain your turns are your decisions, I am almost bound to come fairly close to them — I am pulled beyond myself.

Horst: Ski-ing with somebody else is extremely energizing. You can slip into their energy flow, accept it, adopt it, and simply pattern yourself on it. Ski-ing leads people to a potential predicament which they can get themselves out of, and that in itself is a tremendous accomplishment. So really what we learn more than anything else with ski-ing is knowledge of ourselves.

Ali: As well as that, I think an important aspect is seeing and reacting to what you see. If I'm travelling, for instance, at 30 mph and I want to make a really good curve, I know and can picture exactly how much leg lean I need by the feeling from the back of the ski. I know how much I need to hold the ski on its edge. But if I didn't have some fundamental knowledge of what was happening to the ski I think I wouldn't do as well. It's just that the beginner initially feels no affinity with his skis: they're cumbersome and difficult to walk about in. I think it's only with some understanding of what the ski will do that the beginner's attitude towards his skis changes.

The danger is of becoming so full of technique that we forget one of the most incredible pleasures of ski-ing, which is just simply to run straight through snow and feel it. It's very refreshing for me to come to the United States and see people cruising round having a lot of fun with their feet two feet apart and being very skilful, unlike Europe where people try to ski with their feet jammed together, looking very unskilful and possibly feeling quite unhappy as well.

Horst: I'm not so sure about being totally carefree: to many people ski-ing is a very stylish event and unless they can ski very stylishly and emulate those who act as their models they're not really happy.

As a friend of mine remarked, we delegate the responsibility for health to our doctors; we delegate our spiritual well-being to the churches; and we delegate learning to teachers. We need to take responsibility for these things ourselves and then we'll all be better learners. As I ski moguls, I simply develop a rhythm and then adapt to the moguls as I go. The rhythm is the pendulum of the legs; I simply swing from side to side, allowing them to land softly. I really don't think of a specific technique or style.

Ali: I can't teach anybody my style, but so many people come up to me and say, 'We saw people today and we're sure they learned to ski from you because of the way you ski.' But what is style? All I can hope for is that they understand what they're doing; it's this understanding and their responses which create their own style. I say to whoever comes to me to ski that I'm not going to be able to teach them one thing, But I hope they'll be able to learn a lot.

ARTIFICIAL SLOPES

Sometimes called dry ski slopes. Various types of surface.

Qualified instruction: BASI (British Association of Ski Instructors); ASSI (Artificial Ski Slope Instructors).

Wear old clothes — jeans/cords, long-sleeved shirt/jersey, old anorak, socks, strong gloves, Take your own boots or hire at the slope along with skis and poles.

Check bindings — if in doubt, ask.

Arrive at the slope in time to get yourself organized.

R = Refreshments   T = Tow

This information was correct to the best of our knowledge at the time of printing.

GREATER LONDON AND SOUTH EAST
(Greater London, Surrey, Kent, Sussex)

Alexandra Palace: Alexandra Palace Ski Centre, Alexandra Park (01-888 82284). Skimat, Snomat and Sorbomat 100m, Oct-Mar. RT.

Norwood: Crystal Palace National Sports Centre (01-778 0131). Dendix 32m, Oct-Mar. R.

Uxbridge: Blue Sky Hillingdon Ski Centre, Park Road (Uxbridge 55183). Dendix 130m, & 20m, all year. R, 2Ts

Woolwich: Woolwich Ski Slope, Greenhill Terrace (01-856 5533 ext 853). Dendix 120m & mogul slope, all year. RT.

Esher: Sandown Ski School, Sandown Park, More Lane (Esher 65588). Dendix 100m & Nursery slope, mogul run, all year, summer restricted. RT.

Guildford: Bishop Reindorp School, Larch Avenue (Guildford 37373). Dendix 30m.

Folkestone: Folkestone Sports Centre, Radnor Park Ave (Folkestone 58222). Dendix 45m, all year. RT.

Tunbridge Wells: Bowles Ski Centre, Eridge Green (Crowborough 4127). Dendix 76m, Oct-Mar. RT.

Brighton: Eurosport Slope, 67A North Road (Brighton 688258). Summer Ski 12m, Oct-Apr.

Brighton: North Brighton Adult Education Centre, Carden Ave, Patcham (Brighton 558897).

Newhaven: The Borowski Centre, New Road (Newhaven 5402). Dendix 33m, all year. R.

SOUTHERN
(Berks, Hants, Oxon)

Reading: Carter's Ski Centre, 99 Caversham Road (Reading 55589). Dendix 18m, Oct-Mar.

Aldershot: Stainforth Ski Centre, Hurst Road (Aldershot 25889). Dendix 100m, all year except Jun. RT.

Southampton: Calshot Activities Centre, The Spit, Calshot (Southampton 892077). Dendix 33m, all year except winter/spring hols.R.

Southampton: Southampton Ski Slope, Bassett (Southampton 768732). Dendix 80m & 20m, Sept-Jul. RT.

Carterton: Brize Norton Ski Centre, RAF Brize Norton (Carterton 842924). Dendix 40m & 20m, all year except Jul.

SOUTH WEST
(Glos, Somerset, Devon)

Gloucester: Gloucester Ski Centre, Matson Lane, Robinswood Hill (Gloucester 414300). Dendix 240m & 20m, all year except Christmas Day. R, 2Ts.

Wellington: Wellington Sports Centre, Corams Lane (Wellington 3010). Dendix 50m, all year. R.

Exeter: Exeter & District Ski Club, Clifton Hill Sports Centre (Exeter 211422). Dendix 60m, all year except Aug.

Torquay: Wessex Ski Club, Pontins, Barton Hill (Paignton 25576 day, 33427 night). Dendix 100m, Oct-Apr.

EASTERN
(Essex, Herts, Norfolk, Suffolk)

Basildon: Basildon Ski School, Aquatels Recreation Centre, Cranes Farm Road (Basildon 3377). Dendix 50m.

Brentwood: Warley Ski Centre, Warley Gap (Brentwood 211994). Dendix 90m, 3 nursery slopes, Sep-Jul. RT.

Harlow: Harlow Ski Centre, Hammarskjold Road (Harlow 21792). Dendix 120m, mogul runs, all year. R, 2Ts.

Royston: Bassingbourn Ski Club, Bassingbourn Barracks, Nr Royston (Enquiries: Huntingdon 77363). Dendix 90m, all year. R.

Hemel Hempstead: Herts Ski Centre, S & L Sports, 4 St Albans Hill (Hemel Hempstead 3755). Dendix 150m & Skimat 100m, all year. R, 2Ts.

Watford: Watford Ski School, Woodside Playing Fields, Horseshoe Lane (Garston 676559). Delta 110m & 50m, cross country track 200m, Sep-Jul. RT.

Welwyn Garden City: Welwyn Garden City Ski Slope, Gosling Stadium, Stanborough Road (Welwyn Garden 31056). Skimat 62m, Sep-Apr. RT.

Norwich: Norfolk Ski Club, Whitlingham Lane, Trowse (Norwich 650442). Dendix 100m & 50m, Oct-Mar. T.

Ipswich: Suffolk Ski Club, Bourne Hill (Ipswich 686321). New 1981/82 Sorbo 95m, Sep-Apr but limited summer.

EAST MIDLANDS
(Northants, Notts)

Rushden: Skew Bridge Ski Club, Northampton Road (Rushden 55808). Dendix 115m, Oct-Easter. RT.

Nottingham: Carlton Forum Ski Slope, c/o Golf Range, Foxhill Road, Carlton (Nottingham 872333). Dendix 60m, all year. R.

WEST MIDLANDS
(Staffs, Salop)

Birmingham: Birmingham Ski Schools, c/o 18/19 Snowhill, Queensway (Birmingham 236 6816). Dendix 15m, Sep-Apr. R.

Cradley Heath: Haden Hill Ski Centre, Halesowen Road (Cradley Heath 633833). Dendix 50m, all year except Christmas & Boxing Day. RT.

Wednesday: Tebbutts, 42 High Bullen. (Enquiries: 35 Market Place, Birmingham 556 0802). Sorboski 20m, Oct-Easter. R.

Telford: Telford Ski Slope, Court Street, Madeley (Telford 586791). Dendix 70m, all year. RT.

NORTH WEST
(Cheshire, Lancs, Merseyside)

Bebington: Oval Sports Centre, Old Chester Road (Liverpool 645 0551). Dendix 50m, all year but check. R.

Lancaster Lancaster & Morecambe College of P.E., Morecambe Road (Lancaster 66215 ext 50). Dendix 60m, all year except summer hols.

Clitheroe: Pendle Ski Club, (Clitheroe 25222). Dendix 70m. Oct-Apr. RT.

Manchester: Ellis Brigham Manchester Ski School, Corner Greengate and Chapel Street (Manchester 834 0161). Skimat 33m, Sep-Mar.

Oldham: Ski Counthill, Counthill School, Counthill Road (Manchester 678 4055). Dendix 47m, Sep-Jun. T.

Rossendale: Ski Rossendale, Haslingden Old Road, Rawtenstall (Rossendale 228844). Dendix 180m, 60m & 20m, all year. R, 2Ts.

NORTHERN
(Cumbria, Tyne & Wear, Yorks)

Carlisle: Carlisle and District Ski Club, Edenside (Burgh-by-Sands 562). Dendix, Snomat 50m, Sep-Mar. R.

Workington: West Cumbria Ski Club, Ehenside School, Cleator Moor (Cleator Moor 810306). Dendix 25m, Sep-May.

Sunderland: Silksworth Ski Slope, Silksworth Lane (Sunderland 229119). Dendix 150m, all year, T.

Catterick: Catterick Indoor Ski Slope, Loos Road, Catterick Garrison (Richmond 833788). Skimat 42m, all year. RT.

Harrogate: Harrogate Ski Centre, Hookstone Wood Road (Harrogate 55457). Dendix 110 & 25m, all year. RT.

SCOTLAND
(Aberdeenshire, Angus, Ayrshire; Fife, Inverness-shire, Lothian, Perthshire, Roxburgh, Strathclyde, Stirlingshire)

Aberdeen: Kaimhill Ski Slope, Kaimhill Playfield, Garth Dee Road, Bridge of Dee (Aberdeen 38707). Dendix 85m, all year. R.

Bucksburn: Stonewood Ski Slope, Stoneywood Outdoor Education Centre, 105 Stoneywood Road (Aberdeen 712462). 30m, Sep-Apr.

Glenshee: Glenshee Ski Slope, Cairnwell By Braemar (Braemar 628). Skimat 200m, all year. RT.

Dundee: Ancrum Outdoor Education Resource Centre, 10 Ancrum Road (Dundee 60719). Dendix 60m, Sep-Apr. R.

Arbroath: Royal Marines Condor Camp (Arbroath 72201 ext 110). For Service personnel mainly & ski clubs at other times. Dendix 105m, all year. T.

Newmilns: Irvine Valley Ski Slope, High Street (Kilmarnock 25628). Dendix 80m, RT.

Glenrothes: Fife Institute of P & RE, Viewfield Road (Glenrothes 771770). Snomat 35m, all year. R.

Aviemore: Drambuie Ski Slope, Aviemore Centre (Aviemore 810310). Dendix 50m, summer – closes Nov. RT.

Edinburgh: Hillend Ski Centre, Biggar Road (Edinburgh 445 4433). Dendix 400m, 250m & 30m, all year. RT & chair-lift.

Kinlock Rannoch: Loch Rannoch Hotel, By Pitlochry (Kinloch Rannoch 201 ext 109). Dendix 70m, all year. RT.

Jedburgh: Jedburgh Dry Ski Slope, Jedburgh Anna Complex, The Anna (Jedburgh 2566). Dendix 20m, Aug-Apr. R.

Glasgow: Glasgow Ski Centre, Bellahouston Park, 16 Drumbreck Road (Glasgow 427 4991). Dendix 80m.

Polmont: Polmonthill Ski Centre, Polmont Farm (Polmont 711660). Dendix 100m, all year. RT.

WALES
(Gwynedd, Clywd, Glamorgan, Gwent, Powys)

Betws-y-Coed: Plas y Brenin National Centre for Mountain Activities, Capel Curig (Capel Curig 214). Dendix 70m, all year. RT.

Deeside: Kelsterton College, Connah's Quay (Deeside 817531 ext 269). Delta 40m, Sep-May, RT.

Cardiff: Cardiff Ski Centre, Fairwater Park, Fairwater (Cardiff 561693). Dendix 70m. Sep-Mar. T.

Swansea: Reg Bateman Travel Service Indoor Ski Slope, 1 Prince of Wales Road (Swansea 403350). Dendix 18m, Oct-Mar.

Pontypool: Pontypool Ski Centre, Pontypool Park (Pontypool 56955). Dendix 200m, all year, RT.

Glasbury: Black Mountain Ski Slope, Newcourt, Three Cocks, Brecon (Glasbury 285). Dendix 23m, all year. R.

NORTHERN IRELAND
(Co Armagh)

Craigavon: Craigavon Golf & Ski Centre, Turmoyra Lane, Silverwood, Lurgan (Lurgan 6606). Dendix 75m, all year, RT.

Belfast: P.E. Centre, The Queen's University of Belfast, Botanic Park (Belfast 661111 ext 4317). Nylon 18m, all year. R.

Lisburn: Ulster Ski Club, Llewellyn Ave (Belfast 641326). Dendix 30m, Oct-Apr.

SOUTHERN IRELAND
(Co Dublin)

Kilternan: Ski Club of Ireland, c/o Dublin Sport Hotel (Kilternan 895893). Dendix 180m, Sep-Apr. RT.

MOGUL SLOPES

London: Michael Sobell Sports Centre, Hornsey Road, Islington (01-607 1632). Oct-Mar. R.

Woolwich: Woolwich Ski Slope, Greenhill Terrace (01-856 5533 ext 853). All year.

PRINCIPAL RESORTS

Measurements are given in both metres and feet. Low figures refer to resort altitude, upper figures to highest lift.

AMERICA – EAST COAST

New Hampshire
Cannon Mountain 577 – 1,277m; 1,890 – 4,176ft.

Waterville Valley 464 – 1,183m; 1,520 – 3,870ft.

New York
Hunter Mountain Ski Bowl 489 – 978m; 1,600 – 3,200ft.

Lake Placid 294 – 1,356m; 962 – 4,436ft.

Pennsylvania
Sugarbush Valley 496 – 1,227m; 1,625 – 4,013ft.

Vermont
Killington 672 – 1,290m; 2,200 – 4,220ft.

Mount Snow 504 – 1,087m; 1,650 – 3,556ft.

Stowe 366 – 1,344m; 1,200 – 4,397ft.

Trapp Family Lodge 397 – 917m; 1,300 – 3,000ft.

WEST COAST

California
Heavenly Valley 1,896 – 3,027m; 6,200 – 9,900ft.

Kirkwood 2,385 – 2,996m; 7,800 – 9,800ft.

Mammoth Mountain 2,385 – 3,380m; 7,800 – 11,053ft.

Squaw Valley 1,896 – 2,629m; 6,200 – 8,600ft.

Sugar Bowl 2,104 – 2,563m; 6,881 – 8,383ft.

Colorado
Aspen 2,522 – 3,608m; 8,250 – 11,800ft.

Breckenridge 2,944 – 3,621m; 9,630 – 11,843ft.

Steamboat 2,110 – 3,241m; 6,900 – 10,600ft.

Vail 2,446 – 3,440m; 8,000 – 11,250ft.

Montana
Big Sky 2,293 – 2,996m; 7,500 – 9,800ft.

New Mexico
Taos Ski Valley 2,817 – 3,616m; 9,213 – 11,825ft.

Utah
Park City 2,140 – 3,058m; 7,000 – 10,000ft.

Wyoming
Jackson Hole 1,929 – 3,195m; 6,311 – 10,450ft.

AUSTRIA

Alpbach/Inneralpbach 816 – 1,850m; 2,676 – 6,068ft.

Axams 878 – 2,400m; 2,870 – 7,850ft.

Brand 1,037 – 1,920m; 3,280 – 6,298ft.

Fieberbrunn 792 – 1,642m; 2,600 – 5,380ft.

Finkerberg 847 – 2,101m; 2,772 – 6,873ft.

Gaschurn 1,000 – 2,200m; 3,280 – 7,216ft.

Innsbruck/Igls 582 – 2,343m; 1,909 – 7,685ft.

Ischgl/Galtur 1,377 – 2,884m; 4,518 – 9,397ft.

Kirchberg 772 – 1,979m; 2,525 – 6,470ft.

Kitzbuhel 770 – 1,973m; 2,520 – 6,471ft

Lech/Zurs/Stuben 1,445 – 2,423m; 4,725 – 7,923ft.

Lermoos/Ehrwald 1,009 – 2,210m; 3,300 – 7,200ft.

Mayrhofen 630 – 2,095m; 2,066 – 6,872ft.

Niederau/Oberau 828 – 1,901m; 2,707 – 6,216ft.

Obergurgl/Hochgurgl 1,927 – 3,082m; 6,332 – 10,111ft.

Saalbach 985 – 2,100m; 3,209 – 6,867ft.

Scheffan 754 – 1,655m; 2,467 – 5,414ft.

Schladming/Haus im Ennstal 749 – 2,115m; 2,457 – 6,937ft.

Seefeld 1,200 – 2,064m; 3,936 – 6,770ft.

Serfaus 436 – 749m; 1,425 – 2,449ft.

Slumm 555 – 2,307m; 1,817 – 7,546ft.

Solden/Hochsolden 1,367 – 3,058m; 4,518 – 10,030ft.

Soll/Ellmau 700 – 1,829m; 2,296 – 5,999ft.

St Anton 1,260 – 2,811m; 4,133 – 9,220ft.

St Johann in Tirol 700 – 1,700m; 2,296 – 5,576ft.

Tschagguns 700 – 2,124m; 2,296 – 6,968ft.

Westendorf 800 – 1,892m; 2,625 – 6,208ft.

Zell am See 770 – 2,012m; 2,520 – 6,520ft.

Zell am Ziller 579 – 1,840m; 1,893 – 6,016ft.

CANADA

Alberta
Lake Louise 1,544 – 2,385m; 5,050 – 7,800ft.

Marmot Basin, Jasper 1,651 – 2,616m; 5,400 – 8,557ft.

Norquay/Banff 1,529 – 2,522m; 5,000 – 8,248ft.

Sunshine Village 1,681 – 2,738m; 5,500 – 8,954ft.

Vancouver
Whistler Mountain 305 – 1,308m; 1,000 – 4,280ft.

FRANCE

Alpe d'Huez 1,860 – 3,350m; 6,082 – 10,954ft.

Auran 1,600 – 2,260m; 5,232 – 7,390ft.

Avoriaz 1,795 – 2,467m; 5,870 – 8,070ft.

Barèges 1,240 – 2,050m; 4,054 – 6,703ft.

Chamonix 1,035 – 3,842m; 3,400 – 12,640ft.

Courcheval (Trois Vallées) 1,650 – 1,850m; 5,395 – 6,049ft.

Flaine 1,600 – 2,500m; 5,247 – 8,197ft.

Font Romeu 1,600 – 2,215m; 5,232 – 7,243ft.

Isola 2000 2,000 – 2,610m; 6,540 – 8,534ft.

La Clusaz 1,100 – 2,400m; 3,597 – 7,848ft.

La Mougie 1,800 – 2,245m; 5,886 – 7,341 ft.

La Pierre St Martin 1,650 – 2,000m; 5,395 – 6,540ft.

La Plague 1,930 – 3,250m; 6,332 – 10,660ft.

Le Lioran 1,200 – 1,800m; 3,924 – 5,886ft.

Le Mont-Doré 1,050 – 1,846m; 3,433 – 6,036ft.

Le Sauze 1,400 – 2,400m; 4,578 – 7,848ft.

Les Angles 1,600 – 2,377m; 5,232 – 7,772ft.

Les Arcs 1,610 – 2,800m; 5,281 – 9,184ft.

Les Cauterets 930 – 2,300m; 3,041 – 7,521ft.

Les Deux Alpes 1,655 – 3,531m; 5,414 – 11,549ft.

Les Menuires (Trois Vallées) 1,850 – 2,855m; 6,068 – 9,367ft.

Megève St Gervais 900 – 1,871m; 3,710 – 6,800ft.

Meribel (Trois Vallées) 1,404 – 2,716m; 4,592 – 8,882ft.

Montgenèvre/Clavière 1,360 – 2,691m; 4,461 – 8,826ft.

Morzine 1,000 – 2,460m; 3,270 – 8,044ft.

Orcières 1,830 – 2,655m; 5,984 – 8,681ft.

Porte Puymorens 1,600 – 2,400m; 5,232 – 7,848ft.

Pra-Loup/La Foux d'Allos 1,628 – 2,600m; 5,323 – 8,502ft.

St Lary/Pla d'Adet 1,600 – 2,425m; 5, 248 – 7,954ft.

Tignes 2,107 – 3,669m; 6,892 – 11,999ft.

Valburg 1,670 – 2,010m; 5,460 – 6,562ft.

Val d'Isère 1,850 – 3,459m; 6,068 – 11,346ft.

Val Thorens (Trois Vallées) 2,277 – 3,310m; 7,447 – 10,826ft.

Villard-de-Lans 1,056 – 2,170m; 3,453 – 7,095ft.

Villeneuve 1,380 – 2,483m; 4,512 – 8,119ft.

ITALY

Abbetone 1,400 – 1,982m; 4,578 – 6,481ft.

Aprica 1,180 – 2,575m; 3,870 – 8,448ft.

Bardonecchia 1,315 – 2,815m; 4,303 – 9,206ft.

Bormio 1,225 – 3,020m; 4,108 – 9,906ft.

Cervinia 1,878 – 3,488m; 6,160 – 11,441ft.

Champoluc 1,600 – 2,780m; 5,232 – 9,090ft.

Chiesa 1,000 – 2,363m; 3,279 – 7,748ft.

Cortina d'Ampezzo 1,224 – 3,244m; 4,002 – 10,607ft.

Corvara 1,568 – 2,557m; 5,127 – 8,361ft.

Courmayeur 1,224 – 2,755m; 4,015 – 9,008ft.

Foppolo 1,565 – 2,542m; 5,120 – 8,315ft.

Gressoney 1,642 – 2,736m; 5,371 – 8,947ft.

La Thuile 1,441 – 2,581m; 4,712 – 8,439ft.

La Villa 1,443 – 2,077m; 4,718 – 6,791ft.

Livigno 1,831 – 2,807m; 5,990 – 9,180ft.

Macugnaga 1,350 – 2,900m; 4,414 – 9,512ft.

Madesimo 1,555 – 2,929m; 5,085 – 9,483ft.

Madonna di Campiglio 1,520 – 2,590m; 4,987 – 8,498ft.

Marilleva 1,400 – 1,900m; 4,578 – 6,213ft.

Pila 1,385 – 2,620m; 4,528 – 8,567ft.

San Cassiano 1,537 – 2,003m; 5,025 – 6,549ft.

San Cristina 1,446 – 2,519m; 4,728 – 8,237ft.

Santa Caterina 1,744 – 2,793m; 5,073 – 9,134ft.

Sauze d'Oulx 1,509 – 2,507m; 4,950 – 8,223ft.

Terminillo 1,620 – 2,105m; 5,297 – 6,883ft.

LIECHTENSTEIN

Malbun 1,605 – 2,006m; 5,250 – 6,560ft.

SCOTLAND

Aviemore 550 – 1,100m; 1,800 – 3,600ft.

Glencoe 639 – 1,100m; 2,090 – 3,600ft.

Glenshee 611 – 919m; 2,000 – 3,008ft.

SPAIN

Alto Campos 1,700 – 2,125m; 5,559 – 6,948ft.

Baqueira/Beret 1,500 – 2,500m; 4,905 – 8,175ft.

Candanchu 1,450 – 2,020m; 4,741 – 6,005ft.

Formigal 1,500 – 2,350m; 4,920 – 7,708ft.

La Molina/Masella 1,600 – 2,537m; 5,248 – 8,321ft.

La Tuca 1,050 – 2,250m; 3,433 – 7,357ft.

Panticosa 1,200 – 1,899m; 3,936 – 6,229ft.

Soldeu/Pas de la Casa 1,800 – 2,630m; 5,886 – 8,600ft.

Sol y Nieve 2,100 – 3,470m; 6,867 – 11,347ft.

ANDORRA

1,710 – 2,460m; 5,600 – 8,500ft.

SWITZERLAND

Adelboden/Leuk 1,353 – 2,098m; 4,400 – 7,650ft.

Andermatt 1,447 – 2,961m; 4,731 – 9,682ft.

Anzère 1,500 – 2,500m; 4,920 – 7,913ft.

Arosa 1,745 – 2,653m; 5,900 – 8,700ft.

Bivio 1,776 – 2,731m; 5,807 – 8,930ft.

Braunwald 1,300 – 1,910m; 4,251 – 6,245ft.

Champery 1,055 – 2,284m; 3,450 – 7,470ft.

Champoussin 1,605 – 2,707m; 5,250 – 7,218ft.

Crans Montana 1,470 – 2,927m; 4,985 – 9,969ft.

Davos/Klosters 1,540 – 2,485m; 5,100 – 9,300ft.

Engelberg 1,050 – 3,239m; 3,433 – 10,591ft.

Films Laaz 1,020 – 2,837m; 3,335 – 9,276ft.

Flumerberge 750 – 2,019m; 2,452 – 6,602ft.

Crachen 1,619 – 2,620m; 5,294 – 8,567ft.

Grindelwald 1,039 – 2,495m; 3,400 – 8,160ft.

Gstaad 1,051 – 2,928m; 3,436 – 9,574ft.

Hasliberg 1,061 – 2,245m; 3,469 – 7,341ft.

Interlaken 703 – 1,949m; 2,300 – 6,375ft.

Lenzerheide/Valbella 1,470 – 2,865m; 4,806 – 9,368ft.

Les Diablerets 1,152 – 2,928m; 3,767 – 9,574ft.

Leukerbad 1,401 – 2,889m; 4,581 – 9,447ft.

Leysin/Les Mosses 1,260 – 2,351m; 4,125 – 7,375ft.

Murren 1,651 – 2,974m; 5,400 – 9,725ft.

Saas Fee 1,800 – 3,000m; 5,886 – 9,810ft.

Samnaun 1,731 – 3,034m; 5,600 – 9,921ft.

Sedrun 1,400 – 2,840m; 4,578 – 9,286ft.

Sorenberg 1,166 – 2,350m; 3,812 – 7,684ft.

St Moritz/Pontresina 1,725 – 3,303m; 6,000 – 11,284ft.

Unterwasser 910 – 2,262m; 2,975 – 7,396ft.

Val d'Annivier 1,570 – 2,980m; 5,133 – 9,744ft.

Verbier 1,501 – 3,024m; 4,921 – 9,918ft.

Villars 1,284 – 2,140m; 4,200 – 7,000ft.

Wengen 1,280 – 2,495m; 4,187 – 8,160ft.

Wiler 1,380 – 2,700m; 4,512 – 8,829ft.

Zermatt 1,620 – 3,455m; 5,314 – 11,332ft.

WEST GERMANY

Garmisch-Partenkirchen 670 – 2,966m; 2,190 – 9,698ft.

Oberstdorf 815 – 2,059m; 2,665 – 6,732ft.

The television series was based on *We Learned to Ski* by Harold Evans, Brian Jackman and Mark Ottaway, published by Collins. They describe what helped them to become proficient skiers and analyze resorts and equipment. The book is revised and reprinted regularly as the best-selling book on ski-ing.

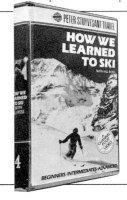

How We Learned to Ski Video Cassette

The Ali Ross instructional materials in the television series is available on video cassette from Peter Stuyvesant Travel, 35 Alfred Place, London WC1E 7DY, price £16.95 inc. p&p.

SELECTED BIBLIOGRAPHY

Abrahams, Horst *Skiing Right (1983)*
Austrian Association of Professional Ski Teachers *The New Official Austrian Ski System* (1958)
BASI Handbook
British Ski Yearbook (1902-71)
Caulfield, Vivian *How To Ski* (1912)
Fedden, Henry R. *Alpine Ski Tour* (1956); *Skiing The Alps* (1958)
Flower, Raymond C. *The Story of Skiing and Other Winter Sports* (1976)
Frazer, Colin *The Avalanche Enigma* (1966); *Avalanches and Safety* (1978)
Georg, H. *Modern Ski Systems* (1954)
Heller, Mark *The World of European Skiing* (1966); *Ski* (1969); *The World Ski Atlas* (1978); *The Skier's Encyclopedia* (1979)
Huber, E. *Complete Ski Manual* (1949)
Kriegel, Bob; Galloway, Tim *Inner Skiing* (1979)
Lunn, Arnold *Skiing* (1913)
Nelson, Denis; Gordon, Sally *Let's Go Ski-ing* (1983)
Riddell, W.J. *Ski Runs of Switzerland (1957); Ski Runs of Austria* (1958)
Riddell, James and Jeanette *Ski Holidays in The Alps* (1961)
Rudiger, Jan *Skiing Skills* (1977)
Sneddon, John *Skilful Skiing* (1982); *Ski Sunday* (1982)
Witherall, Warren *How the Racers Ski* (1972)
Williams, Berry *Where to Ski* (1974)

ACKNOWLEDGEMENTS

We gratefully acknowledge the help of the Ski Club of Great Britain (118 Eaton Square, London SW1 W9AF, 01-235 4711) in providing information for the list of artificial slopes.

Our thanks to the United States Travel and Tourism Administration for the photograph of Vail on p21; and to the Swiss National Tourist Office for the photographs of Wengen on p20.

Design and Editorial Coordination:
Graham Davis Associates
Art Director: Graham Davis
Designer: Kevin Ryan

Illustrators: Roger Coldwell, Chris Forsey, James Macdonald,
Origination: Wace Gee & Watson Ltd.
Photographers: Harry Evans, Jon Lane, Heinz Muller, John Price Studios
Photographic printing: Geoff Goode Photographics Ltd.
PMT Services: Smith/Brown Partnerships
Retouching and artwork: Andy Earl
Typesetting: Text Filmsetters Ltd (Orpington)

Morgan car (page 53) loaned by John Bitten Garages, Arkley, Herts.
Sportswear: Event of London
Skis: Rossignol G.B.
Boots and Bindings: Salomon G.B.